Table of Contents

HICK'S LAW AND DECISION MAKING

In the field of user experience (UX) design, there is a fundamental rule known as the Hick-Hyman Law, commonly referred to as Hick's Law, named after an American psychologist Ray Hyman and his colleague William Edmund Hick. This law places emphasis on the link between the quantity of options consumers are given and how long it takes them to decide. Ten lamps were randomly lighted in an experiment by Hick and Hyman. The illuminated lamp was available for participants to select. Participants had more time to make the proper decision as more lamps were lighted. In essence, Hick's Law emphasizes one's capacity for making choices under various levels of uncertainty, and a number of options causes decision time to increase logarithmically.

HICK'S LAW FORMULA

$RT = a + b \times \log2 (n)$

A reaction time is **RT**. It is the interval of time between the onset of a stimulus and the beginning of the response. Different types of reaction time exist, including simple reaction time, which is relevant to simple possible responses, and choice reaction time, which occurs when multiple stimuli are presented but only one must be chosen. Quick decisions and actions are subject to Hick's Law. The formula's constants are **a** and **b**. They are reliant on the specific task and the conditions for task response. The number of options are given as **n**. The relationship between the quantity of stimuli and the user's response to each stimulus can be used to calculate reaction time.

Pictorial representation of Hick's law formula

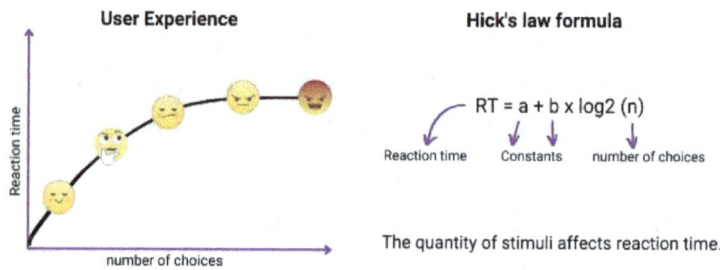

Applying Hick's law to UX

Hick's Law can be applied in practically every circumstance where users must make straightforward selections. UX designers can enhance website navigation using Hick's Law, streamline the login and checkout process, add categories, and remove all but the most essential options. Hick's Law can speed up consumer decision-making and enhance their experience with your product as a whole. I advise looking at the ways Hick's Law can be used to enhance user experience. Using Hick's Law, fewer options are offered to users. Businesses frequently think that providing as many choices as possible will draw in more customers. When given more options, visitors typically take longer to decide; decreasing the number of options shortens this time.

Human psychology is the foundation of Hick's Law. When faced with a variety of possibilities, people attempt to process and assess each one in order to make the optimal decision. If users are presented with too many options, they may become paralyzed by their choices. This occurs when a choice is over thought or overanalyzed, resulting in a decision being postponed or never made. Hick's Law instructs UX designers to reduce the quantity of options and aid consumers in making selections quickly.

The home page for the Google search engine is my favorite illustration of simplicity. Take a look at the changes since the 1998 debut. It is a wonderful illustration of keeping things straightforward.

Google Search   I'm Feeling Lucky

Current Goggle homepage

Compare the current page to the search engine's original homepage, which debuted in September 1998.

Goggle homepage 1998 (source Goggle)

Google!

Search the web using Google!

10 results ▾   Google Search   I'm feeling lucky

Index contains ~25 million pages (soon to be much bigger)

About Google!

Stanford Search Linux Search

Get Google! updates monthly!

your e-mail   Subscribe   Archive

Copyright ©1997-8 Stanford University

You can use these three methods to simplify the interface and cut down on the number of options.

1. Establish categories.

Create categories for your menu items if you have a lot of them. Even if you have a lot of categories, individuals benefit from organization. See how businesses have been utilizing Hick's Law to simplify decisions for users for years so you can learn from the experts. For instance, Zappos has organized millions of products into manageable categories so that you can easily find what you're looking for.

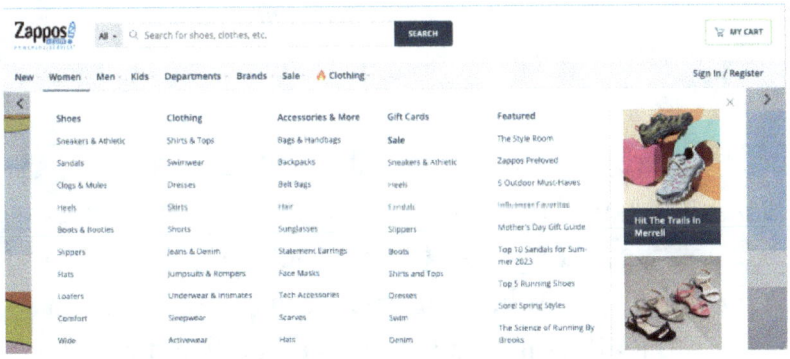

Zappos establishing categories for millions of product (source: Zappos.com)

2. Sort the most crucial alternatives into priority order.

As a UX designer, your job is to identify the features that consumers require and guide them to the most likely choices so they can make a choice. For instance, Zappos offers "Popular categories on sale" in addition to the regular menu with categories to grab your attention and help you make a decision.

Shop Popular Categories On Sale

(source: Zappos.com)

There are a colossal amount of categories and products on Amazon. To prevent overwhelming users, they categorize the products you've previously searched for or purchased and present the most alluring and advantageous discounts, tailoring their suggestions to the kinds of goods you're interested in.

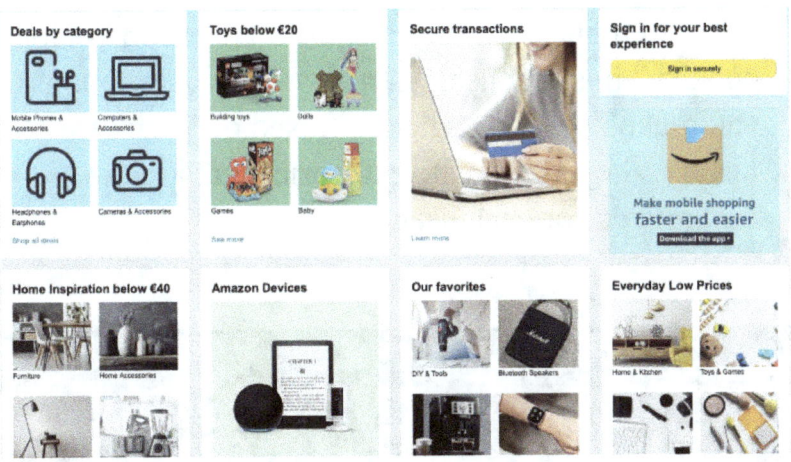

(Source Amazon.com)

Despite having a collection of more than 5,000 films and television shows, Netflix is aware of how difficult it is for customers to decide which content to watch. Just about how many different genres there are and how much time and effort it would require to go through them all.

Genres ▼		
Action & Adventure	Dramas	Romance
Anime	Dutch	Scandinavian
British	European	Sci-Fi & Fantasy
Celebrating Disability with Dimension	Horror	Science & Nature
Comedies	International	Teen
Crime	Kids	Thriller
Docuseries	Reality & Talk	US

(Source: Netflix)

Netflix emphasized the category "Top 10 in your country" to assist users narrow down their options and make decisions quickly. Based on watch history, they also create categories that are customized for each user.

(Source: Netflix)

3. Convert complicated activities into straightforward ones.

Consider each step as it comes. The user experience will be improved by splitting challenging activities up into smaller pieces. The use of several phases in the checkout process for purchasing products is the best illustration of this procedure. A succession of screens with a few options can be made in place of a lengthy checkout form. Multiple phases can be used to streamline a tedious checkout procedure, increasing the likelihood that customers will finish their purchases. We refer to this as progressive disclosure. Take a look at how Ikea broke down the checkout procedure into three easy steps:

(Source: IKEA)

USING PROGRESSIVE DISCLOSURE TO GRADUALLY REVEAL OPTIONS

Co-founder of the Nielsen Norman Group and proponent of progressive disclosure, Jakob Nielsen, first proposed the concept. Applications become less mistake prone and easier to learn because to this interface design style. Jakob Nielsen took into account the fact that people want choices that are both straightforward and comprehensive enough to suit all of their demands. Progressive disclosure can satiate both of these conditions.The "Learn more" button is a clear illustration of progressive disclosure in action. When you use progressive disclosure, you first enter the most crucial details or choices, and then additional choices are displayed in the input field in the order of their labels.

Let's look at some instances to discover where and how progressive disclosure might be used.

Taking into account alternative methods of sharing information

Not all decisions need to be made quickly and simply. For instance, it's crucial to understand the user's viewpoint or the specifics of the issue if you ask for feedback. To obtain more information from the user in this situation, you can leave the standard selections alone and add a "other" option.Coursera provides a simple form that may be used to rate a course with just one click. Users only need to select the star count. They may choose to write their thoughts.

Your review

Write your review (optional)

By clicking Submit, I agree that my feedback may be viewed
by the Coursera community, in compliance with the
Coursera Terms of Use and My Profile privacy settings.

Submit

(Source: Coursera)

Progressive disclosure is used by Google in the
"People also ask" section. You may learn more
about the subject by clicking on the question.

People also ask ⋮

What is an example of a progressive disclosure UX? ⌄

What is a progressive level of disclosure? ⌄

What is progressive disclosure of form fields? ⌄

What are design principles in UX? ⌄

What are the 4 D's of UX? ⌄

What are the 5 levels of UX strategy? ⌄

Feedback

(Source: Goggle)

Progressive disclosure in dropdown menus

It's preferable to hide navigation options when there are a lot of them in the menu to avoid confusing consumers with unrelated information.

Apple's website has a modern, minimalistic design.

Source: Apple.com

But if you tap the required category, you'll find all the alternatives you require.

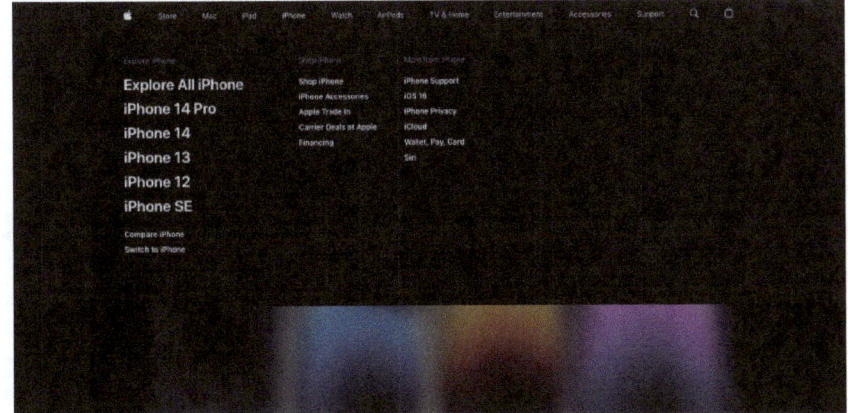

Source: Apple.com

Progressive disclosure in carousels

Using sliders or carousels to display your products engages customers and encourages interaction. Users can learn about new or associated products with your assistance. Amazon employs this technique successfully.

Source: Amazon.com

CREATING INSTRUCTIONS AND LABELING WITH CLARITY AND CONCISENESS

Let's talk about forms, which are one of the most important aspects of the user experience. Forms are used to gather user data. Forms should be straightforward and easy to use if you want to make a positive impression on your users.

Utilize Hick's Law to make forms simpler

In sign-in and checkout forms, it's critical to limit the options. We should steer clear of several time-consuming stages that can deter users from signing up or making a purchase. We lose potential users when sign-in forms are confusing or overwhelming. Purchasing-wise, the more steps, the higher the rate of cart abandonment. Reduce the number of options on forms and include straightforward instructions to improve the user experience for visitors.

Canva allows users to register for the site with only one click by using social media.

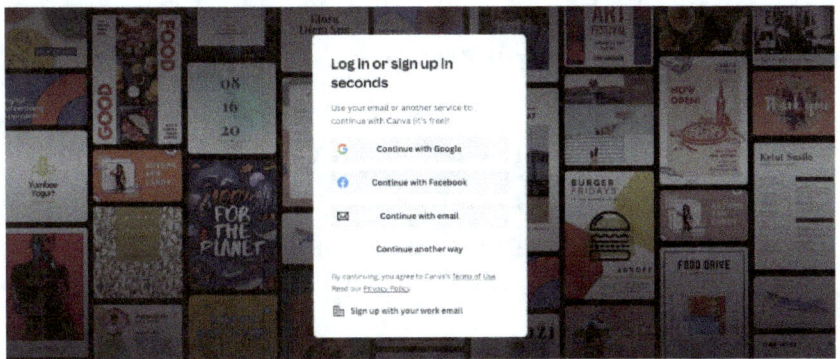

Source: Canva.com

Language that is clear and simple can assist users finish the task and understand the data they need to supply. Users shouldn't be allowed to assume or enter data that they are unsure of. Users comprehend activities better when information is presented logically. Your queries ought to go from simple to difficult.

A form that satisfies the following requirements is probably going to get more submissions and conversions:

1. Only add necessary fields
Limit the number of fields you add: Remember, speedier conclusions come from fewer options.

2. Compose concise, thorough labels

A label, which is a brief text description of an input field, icon, or button, is used. It is preferable to add labels to form fields so that everyone can access them, even if what you are entering appears apparent to you.Do not replace labels in the input field with placeholder characteristics, however you can add them as well.

3. Include logically connected fields.

If your form asks about two distinct topics, put the parts in different fields. Put them in line if they are connected.

4. Include a progress bar.

A progress indicator would be ideal if your form has more than one stage.

5. Make fields a single column.

A single-column form is often more efficient since it looks simpler and makes it easier for users to complete it fast and easily without missing any fields.

Reducing the number of options can help consumers save time, which is important. That is the main idea behind Hick's Law. A UX designer's primary responsibility is striking the correct balance between utility and simplicity. An accessible navigation system, effective forms, and a pleasant user experience are all components of user-friendly design. Therefore, Hick's Law is crucial in the realm of user experience.

FITTS'S LAW AND INTERACTION DESIGN

Fitts' Law is a cornerstone of user interface design and human-computer interaction theory. It offers insightful information on how users interact with graphical user interfaces (GUIs) and demonstrates how interactive element placement and size can be optimized by designers. Paul Fitts, a psychologist, developed a predictive model in 1954 that illustrates how rapidly people can choose a goal. The user is attempting to engage with a target. It can be a form field that has to be filled out or a button that needs to be tapped. In human-computer interaction, this model is frequently employed.

Fitts' Law states that it takes longer for a user to acquire a target the farther away it is and the smaller it is. Small, distant targets have the largest interaction costs, whereas large, nearby objects have the lowest interaction costs.

INTERACTION COSTS

Interaction costs are "the sum of efforts—mental and physical—that users must deploy in interacting with a site to achieve their goals," according to The Nielsen Norman Group. Therefore, a user incurs no interaction cost if they are able to obtain the information they need without having to scroll, tap, or otherwise investigate. There will be a higher interaction cost if a user must locate a menu, navigate through more than a dozen selections, then click a tiny button to submit their form. UX and UI designers prefer to keep these expenses to a minimum. Their app is more usable the lower the cost of interaction. By adhering to Fitts' Law and minimizing attention switches, reading, scrolling, clicking, typing, waiting for pages to load, attention switches, memory load, and exploring to uncover pertinent information, designers can reduce interaction costs.

Fitts' Law's mathematical expression is:

$$T = a + b \cdot \log_2(1 + D/W)$$

- The movement's completion time is denoted by **T**.

- Constants **a** and **b** are determined empirically.

- The distance between the starting location and the target is **D**.

- **W** denotes the target's width or size.

Typical applications of Fitts's Law

Fitts' Law is among the psychological design concepts that is most frequently disregarded.

Here are a few instances of it in use:

- A close-by button that executes an action near the active elements
- Important elements have been enlarged for ease of selection.
- The shortest interactive lists conceivable
- The quickest route to the targeted CTA
- On desktops and mobile devices, menus are located at the upper corners of the screen, respectively.

How does UI design relate to Fitts's Law?

Basically, any interface that uses a mouse or finger may be seen applying this approach. In order to determine the right sizes for interactive elements, the ideal places for them, and to identify potential usability difficulties, it is used in user interface design. Fitts' Law incorporates security, practicality, and usability into UI design. When it comes to heavy machinery safety measures, the shutdown button is typically bigger, redder, and simpler to press than the startup button. Mobile apps that make their login buttons fit within the thumb zones are convenient.

Website buttons are often large, and menus are typically found in the upper corners of your screen thanks to Fitts's Law. By strategically positioning important calls to action adjacent to relevant forms or headlines, UI designers may instruct users what to do. Users will expect to see them here and can click them with little effort.

Concepts of Fitts' Law for UI Design

Size: It's usually advisable to aim for larger targets. Consider using big, clearly delineated, and fully clickable items.

Distance: Restrict movement to a minimum. Consider the distance between buttons, place crucial activities in the thumb and prime pixel zones, and shorten the distance between elements that perform comparable functions. The Gestalt principle of proximity can be compared to this.
Effort: Make use of magic and prime pixels. Make your interactive components simple to click and locate.

What exactly is a prime pixel?

When a user opens a website or program, their pointer is at the prime pixel on the screen. It is the location from which the user will perform all of their tasks. Right-click menus were created because they are logically closest to the primary pixel. The prime pixel on a mobile device is the spot where your thumbs tend to rest. The thumb zones are another name for them. On your iPhone, you'll see that menus are typically located where your thumbs rest at the bottom of the screen.

Designers should aim to place all of their desired calls to action as near to that point as they can. Because the user's beginning point is typically different each time, the prime pixel isn't entirely predictable. When predicting the precise prime pixel is next to impossible, it is possible to anticipate the likely prime pixel based on the user's activities when interacting with your application. I'll give you three instances of that:

- The search button is always next to the Google search bar, which is always in the center of the screen.
- Logins are typically found in the navigation's upper right corner on websites.
- Normally, forms are in the center of the page, with a sizable "submit" button at the bottom.

How do magic pixels work?

The four corners, top edge, and bottom edge of a screen are all examples of magic pixels. Boundaries are created by the magic pixels. Beyond these points, your cursor cannot move. They are nearly always the ones that are the furthest from the primary pixel. Because they can't foresee the prime pixel, designers employ conventions like the middle of the screen, the corners, and the thumb zones on mobile as a reference for the best placement. You'll learn by employing tactics like the Rule of Thirds that having a uniform website that's simple to navigate is just as crucial as being close to CTAs. Magic pixels are often reserved for standard operations because to their great distance from the prime pixel. The upper corners of your screen have buttons for quit, minimize, account controls, log in, and full-screen.

The screen's corners and edges are always in the same spot and are immovable, even though they aren't frequently close to the prime pixel. They can be rapidly reached because of this. The corners of the screen won't be utilized by web designers as effectively as they can by native user interfaces. They therefore rely on the second-best magic zone, which is the screen's middle.

UI DESIGN EXAMPLES USING FITTS' LAW

Spotify

Users of Spotify's desktop application can access frequently used features via the right-click menu. As a result, the prime pixel is virtually always used to its full potential. To access their most frequently performed tasks, a user doesn't even need to move their mouse from its initial position.

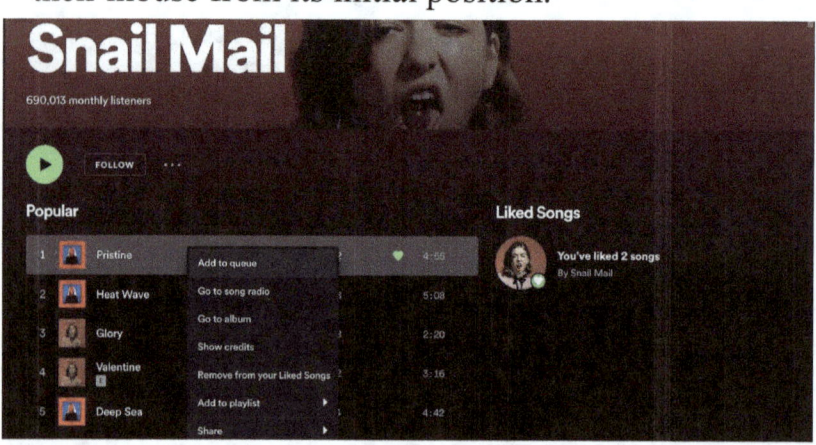

Source: Spotify

Nest

An excellent illustration of Fitts' law is the Nest thermostat.

Source: Nest

This prediction model suggests that pie menus are more effective. However, in favor of simpler-to-design linear menus, this notion is largely disregarded. Nest's device interface embraces the pie menu. Despite its small size, the complete machine may be operated with just two gestures and very minimal human engagement.

iPHONE

iPhone introduced a new shutdown method in response to reports of users' iPhones shutting off unintentionally while in their pockets.These actions operate somewhat in opposition to Fitts' law. High engagement costs make it difficult for a user to unintentionally shut off an iPhone. The "slide to power off" function must be slid after the user presses two buttons to trigger the shutdown screen.It is more probable that the user will cancel out rather than shut down because the cancel button is located at the bottom of the screen and is quicker to tap.

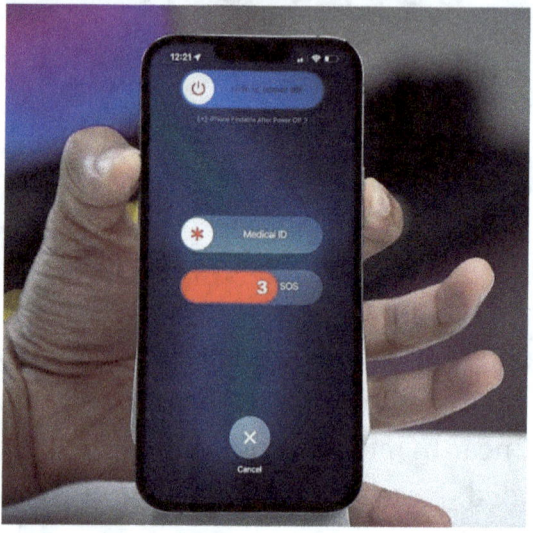

iphone shutdown menu

Goggle

Google places its menu selections in the upper corners and its search area in the middle of the screen. This makes use of prime and maybe magic pixels. A good example of a mental model is the "Google Search" button, which is placed just beneath the search input area and may be clicked on throughout. "I'm Feeling Lucky," a comparable button that is hierarchically categorized, is located just next to the "Google Search" button.

Source: Goggle

Fitts' Law is a fantastic place to start when developing usability criteria, although it's not always accurate. Never underestimate the power of data over theory. Testing your design on actual users is the greatest approach to determine whether it is user-friendly. Asking questions and looking for a deeper understanding of why something is working is always good. Think practically about what you're applying that to in the actual world after using theory as a starting point. These so-called "laws" are really recommendations that should not be blindly followed. Think about the placement of the calls to action on your website or application, how you space and size your buttons, and where you might reduce interaction costs.

GESTALT PRINCIPLES AND VISUAL PERCEPTION

Gestalt principles, which direct us through the complex realm of perception and aesthetics, are the unsung heroes of visual design. Gestalt principles provide a set of recommendations that aid users in making sense of the digital world they come into contact with, much like Jakob's Law, which emphasizes the value of familiarity. In this chapter, we'll look at how these psychologically based concepts influence how we think about design and improve user experiences.

Important Takeaways

- Patterns of Perception: Gestalt principles are based on the ways in which people intuitively arrange and process visual data. Understanding these patterns can help designers make interfaces that are more useful and aesthetically pleasing.

- Simplicity and Clarity: The principles encourage simplicity and clarity in design, making sure that users can easily understand how information is organized and how elements relate to one another. Gestalt principles assist designers in achieving visual harmony, which fosters an attractive and well-balanced design.

Overview

Creating a cohesive and appealing visual experience is crucial in the field of design. Every day, users engage with a vast array of digital interfaces, and how well they can immediately understand and interact with these interfaces can make or break their experience. Gestalt concepts apply in this situation. Gestalt principles are fundamentally a set of laws that define how individuals perceive and arrange visual elements and are derived from human psychology. They demonstrate how the visual world naturally appeals to our brains' desire for clarity, coherence, and significance. Designers may produce interfaces that complement users' cognitive processes and make interactions easier and more intuitive by comprehending and utilizing these ideas.

Clarity and Simplicity

The Law of Prägnanz, which argues that humans typically perceive complicated shapes as simple and well-organized, is one of the core Gestalt concepts. This idea promotes clarity and simplicity in design. An interface's structure and content should be easy for users to understand. This is accomplished by:

- Grouping: Elements that are connected or have a similar function should be arranged visually. For instance, a navigation menu should contain groups of navigation links.

- Similarity: Items that have similar visual characteristics, such as color, shape, or size, are seen as a unit. This idea aids in establishing uniformity throughout an interface.

Visual symmetry

Another crucial Gestalt element is the Law of Continuity. It implies that instead of sudden transitions, individuals like to perceive continuous, smooth lines or patterns. This idea can be used by designers to harmonize the appearance of user interfaces. For instance:

- Flow: Organize items to create a logical flow that will lead consumers through a procedure or a story. A seamless user journey is facilitated by fluid transitions and thoughtful layouts.

- Alignment: To establish a sense of order and alignment, elements should be aligned both horizontally and vertically. Alignment correctly improves reading and appearance.

Closure and accomplishment

Common Fate and Closure are examples of notions covered by the Gestalt principles. While Common Fate argues that pieces going in the same direction are viewed as belonging together, Closure suggests that users have a tendency to mentally complete incomplete shapes. To improve an interface's visual appeal, use the following guidelines:

- Iconic Design: Icons frequently depend on the user's aptitude for mentally completing shapes or recognizing spartan representations. Making intuitive icons is made easier by being familiar with these principles.

- Animation: Take into account the Common Fate idea when implementing animations. A clear message is more likely to be delivered when elements move in unison.

Origin

Early 20th-century gestalt psychology, which gave rise to these ideas, developed in reaction to the study of human perception. It aimed to comprehend how individuals instinctively arrange visual components into significant wholes. Since then, design theory has incorporated this information as a fundamental component, helping designers create interfaces that connect with consumers on a subconscious level. Gestalt principles provide designers with a thorough understanding of how users perceive and engage with visual information, to sum up. Designers may create interfaces that not only look good but also offer a more user-friendly and delightful experience by adhering to these principles and aiming for simplicity, clarity, and visual harmony. Gestalt principles highlight the underlying human desire for coherence and meaning in design, ultimately strengthening the world of digital interfaces, just as Jakob's Law highlights the significance of familiarity.

APPLYING GESTALT PRINCIPLES

Gestalt principles, which have their roots in human psychology, provide designers with a strong framework for producing visually appealing and understandable user interfaces. Designers may create designs that captivate consumers, speed up information processing, and improve the overall user experience by comprehending and putting these ideas into practice. Here are some useful examples of how you might use Gestalt ideas in your design work:

1. Proximity: Group Related Elements Together

According to Gestalt's Law of Proximity, things that are arranged close together are seen as a group. This idea can be used in a variety of situations:

- Navigation Menus: A navigation menu should group together links that are linked to one another. Show that they belong to the same category by placing them next to one another.

- Form Fields: To clearly show the relationship between labels and input fields, arrange them side by side on forms. Users will be able to identify each label's associated field with ease.

2. Similarity: Use Consistency in Design

According to Gestalt's Law of Similarity, objects with similar characteristics (such as color, shape, or size) are seen as belonging together. Utilize this idea to establish consistency:

- Button Styles: Maintain consistency in the color, shape, and size of your buttons across your interface. Users will easily relate this style to objects that can be clicked.

- Icon Sets: Maintain visual coherence while utilizing icons. To strengthen their relationship, icons with identical meanings ought to have similar aesthetic characteristics.

3. Conclude by Encouraging Completion

According to Gestalt's Law of Closure, people have a tendency to mentally finish off incomplete shapes. Use this idea to create interesting and imaginative design:

- Logos: Create logos or graphic components that, despite missing parts, convey a full shape. By doing this, people' imaginations are piqued and a memorable image is produced.

- Even if the loading process is not totally circular, including loading animations that imply a circular or complete movement. It gives users a sense of advancement.

4. Continuity: Guide User's Eye

According to Gestalt's Law of Continuity, users favor smooth, continuous patterns. Use these design principles to direct users through your interface:

- Flow and Layout: Establish a logical flow in your design by placing the material in a hierarchical or chronological order, for example. Users will naturally follow the route you've set up.

- Diagonal Lines: Connect similar pieces by using diagonal lines or other visual signals. This may direct users' attention in a particular manner.

5. Common Fate: Emphasize Interaction

Objects going in the same direction are viewed as belonging together, according to Gestalt's Law of Common Fate. Apply the following rule to interactive elements:

- Animation: Add animations to items that are connected and perform the same action. For instance, when a user hovers over a button, related elements like tooltips or pop-ups should animate simultaneously.

- Progress Indicators: Show progress counters that update as the page loads. These metrics will be linked to the ongoing action by users.

6. Figure-Ground: Create Visual Hierarchy

The separation between the main topic (figure) and the backdrop (ground) is emphasized by the figure-ground principle. Apply the following rule to create a visual hierarchy:

- Contrast: Use color, size, or contrast to make your main content or call-to-action elements stand out. This highlights the most crucial components for users.

- Whitespace: Effectively separate content from the background by using whitespace. It improves clarity and readability.

Gestalt concepts can be applied to design in order to enhance user engagement and comprehension in addition to aesthetic appeal. Designers may improve their interfaces for better usability and user happiness by studying how users organize and process visual information.

VISUAL HIERARCHY AND LAYOUT DESIGN

Fundamental concepts in the fields of graphic design, web design, and user experience (UX) design include visual hierarchy and layout design. They are essential in directing users' attention, effectively communicating information, and designing aesthetically beautiful and user-friendly interfaces. In this extensive note, we'll explore the definitions, guiding concepts, methods, and real-world applications of visual hierarchy and layout design.

An Overview of Visual Hierarchy

The arrangement and presentation of elements inside a design to denote their significance and direct the viewer's eye are known as visual hierarchy. It creates an ordered order for people to engage and comprehend content. For numerous reasons, visual hierarchy is important:

1. Communication: It facilitates effective and speedy dissemination of the primary message or the hierarchy of the information to users.

2. Engagement: A strong visual hierarchy draws viewers in and entices them to examine the information more thoroughly.

3. Usability Logical element organization improves user experience by making the interface more intuitive and simple to use.

Important Components of Visual Hierarchy:

- Size: Elements that are larger tend to attract more attention. Secondary or supporting parts might be smaller, but important content should be larger.

- Color: Eye-catching hues might be bright or contrasting. To emphasize important details, use color judiciously.

- Typography: The appearance of text is influenced by the typeface, font size, and formatting (bold, italics). The styles of the body text, subheadings, and headers should be different.

- Position: Elements positioned in the top or middle of a layout are usually the ones that catch the eye first. Positioning is also influenced by the intended audience's reading orientation.

- Spacing: Proper spacing between items fosters a sense of order and makes it easier for users to distinguish between them.

Guidelines for Visual Hierarchy:

1. Using the F- and Z-patterns Users frequently scan content in an F-pattern (top to bottom, left to right) or Z-pattern (diagonal scan), according to studies. With these patterns in mind, create layouts that place key content along these paths.

2. The "Golden Ratio" A mathematical idea called the "golden ratio" is applied in design to produce proportions that look attractive to the eye. To establish balance and harmony, it can be utilized to layout design.

3. Alignment and Grids: Aligning pieces consistently and using grids make sure that they are rationally arranged, which enhances the visual hierarchy as a whole.

4. In contrast To draw attention to important parts, use contrast in the form of color, size, or font. These features stand out and grab consumers' attention thanks to contrast.

Layout Design: An Overview

The arrangement and organization of visual components, text, and multimedia within a certain space, such as a web page, print publication, or mobile app screen, is referred to as layout design. A good layout design takes both usefulness and aesthetics into account. Layout design must take the following factors into account:

1. White space Whitespace, also referred to as negative space, is the space between and around objects in a layout. It creates breathing space, improves readability, and helps create a simple, uncluttered style.

4. Balance: Depending on the desired effect, distribute elements equitably or asymmetrically to achieve visual balance.

No area of the layout will feel overwhelmed or ignored thanks to balance.

5. Consistency: Maintaining consistency in layout design fosters a sense of predictability and order. It comprises using fonts, colors, space, and alignment consistently.

6. Alignment: Using proper alignment makes sure that pieces are connected and arranged visually. Depending on the objectives of the design, alignment can be justified, centered, left-aligned, or right-aligned.

7. Grid Systems: Grids are frameworks that aid in the organization of content. They offer a framework for arranging components in a unified, aesthetically acceptable way.

8. Responsive Design: Responsive design is necessary in the modern digital world. Creating layouts that adjust to different screen sizes and devices is necessary to guarantee a consistent user experience.

Guidelines for Layout Design:

1. Emphasize: Apply visual hierarchy concepts to draw attention to the layout's most crucial information or components.

2. Unity: By ensuring that every component functions in harmony with one another, you may create a sense of coherence and oneness. There should be a common theme or goal among the elements.

3. Flow: Use a logical flow to lead consumers through the layout. Think about how your target audience reads (for example, left to right or right to left).

4. Accessibility: Make sure that your design is user-friendly for everyone, including people with impairments. Use readable font sizes, appropriate titles, and alt text for photos.

Practical Applications:

1. Web Design: To provide a simple and interesting user experience, navigation menus, headlines, graphics, and call-to-action buttons must be placed according to visual hierarchy and layout design.

2. Printing Design Layout design determines how text and graphics are arranged to efficiently and artistically convey information in print items like brochures and magazines.

3. Mobile App Design: Visual hierarchy is essential for displaying content in a clear and succinct manner in mobile apps due to the restricted screen real estate.

4. User interface and user experience (UI/UX Design) To make sure that digital products are user-friendly, intuitive, and aesthetically pleasing, designers rely on layout design and visual hierarchy.

Visual hierarchy and layout design are crucial components of every designer's arsenal, to sum up. They are the unseen hands that lead people around the physical and digital worlds, facilitating access to information and engaging interactions. Designers may build designs that not only draw attention but also successfully connect with users and improve their experience by mastering these ideas and methods.

MILLER'S LAW AND INFORMATION INTERPRETATION

What is Miller's Law, first off?

George Miller, an American psychologist and one of the founding fathers of cognitive psychology and, more broadly, cognitive science, came up with Miller's Law in 1956.He was interested in our ability to make decisions using our "working memory," or the capability of the brain to hold several pieces of information simultaneously. Miller's Law is frequently referred to as the "Magical Number Seven, Plus or Minus Two." According to this guideline, an individual can hold and comprehend around seven pieces of information at once (plus or minus two). Beyond this limit, cognitive overload sets in, making it difficult to efficiently process and retain knowledge.

Implications for Information Interpretation:

The presentation, arrangement, and interpretation of information are significantly affected by Miller's Law:

1. Chunking Information: To make information easier to understand, it must be divided into sensible "chunks." For instance, phone numbers are broken up into groups of digits (e.g., 555-123-4567) to make them easier to remember.

2. Prioritizing Key aspects: It's important to provide the most important aspects first when communicating information. Miller's Law advises communicators and designers to concentrate on the main idea rather than saturate the audience with details.

3. Reducing Cognitive Load: The amount of mental work needed to process information is referred to as cognitive load. By presenting knowledge in digestible portions, designers and educators can lessen cognitive load by following Miller's Law.

Now that we are aware of what it is, how does it actually operate?

Miller discovered through carefully designed tests that raising the quantity of "bits" of information above this point leads to confusion and erroneous judgments. The "channel capacity" was what he named this moment.

The mysterious number seven

This means that, during a particular time window, roughly seven bits can be reliably transferred over a channel (your short-term memory). This can be easily remembered by using the enchanted number seven. So far, so easy, Miller had tested the rule of seven and found that it worked as predicted. However, one thing worried me. Miller discovered that the seven-second memory span held true for a wide variety of material. For instance, seven words with numerous letters each put as much of a strain on the brain as seven single-digit numbers. He developed a novel theory known as "chunks" to account for this behavior.

How do chunks work?

Miller came to the notion that chunks, not bits, of information might fit into the memory. He described a chunk as the most significant or recognizable informational item within a larger collection of materials. As a result, the definition of a chunk is arbitrary; its content is determined by the test taker's level of education. For a natural speaker, a word might be one chunk, for instance.

However, this identical word would most likely appear as a collection of pieces to someone who is completely new with the language.

Could I get your phone number?
This is valid for memorizing lengthy groups of numbers, such as the digits on your phone. Try this simple exercise: Read these numbers and see if you can memorize them.

087182349

Try to remember the order while you are closed-eyed. Struggling? Now try it once again using this format:

(087) 182-349

You should discover that this grouping or chunking actually helps your brain's ability to retain information quickly.

What does this mean for UX design, though?
Miller's Law and user experience design:
Every time you open an app on your phone or visit a website, your brain starts a learning process. Virtual carts, graphic carousels, and dynamic menus all rely on the brain's capacity to learn, navigate, and stay focused in order to accomplish a

task. Each unnecessary click, awkward navigational step, or perplexing command increases the cognitive strain. Our seven (plus or minus two) things are stored and processed in our working memory, which gets progressively more congested. The brain's function starts to slow down as it processes more information than it can process, decision-making becomes hampered, and at worst tasks may be abandoned. When performing such tasks, the brain will inevitably experience some level of cognitive burden. In order to best serve the user, the designer must anticipate and take into account the constraints of how the mind functions.

Avoiding these common problems will prevent working memory overload:

- Too many choices
- Not enough clarity
- Too many considerations needed

Large menus, lengthy item lists, an excess of design elements, and substantial textual material are examples of common mistakes that can result in information overload and raise your bounce rate. Instead, prioritize clarity, cut down on options, avoid confusing iconography, and remove any extraneous parts and duties. Users will experience less cognitive strain as a result.

Let's now examine several instances of Miller's Law in operation.

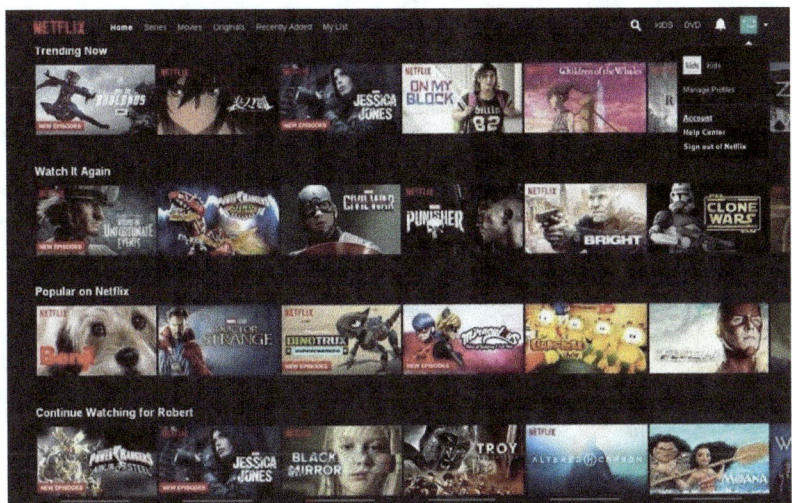

Netflix Homepage (source: Netflix)

The original streaming platform appears to have chosen six as its magic number. On the site, each menu and carousel is displayed as a separate chunk with six options. The website carefully adheres to Miller's suggested restrictions, down to the horizontally chunked rows of icons indicating "Trending Now" or "Popular on Netflix" and the main navigation button. The last four shows are hidden even in the blatantly numbered list of the "Top 10 Shows in the U.S. Today" that appears.

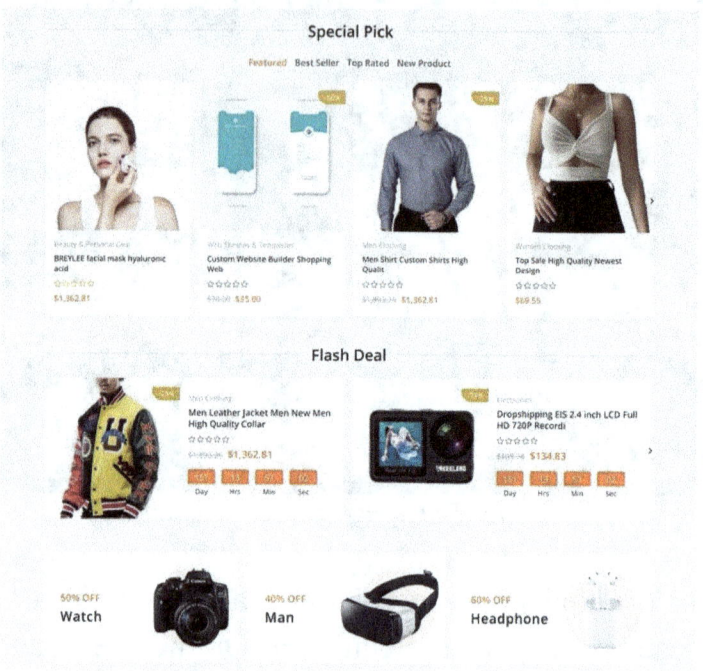

eBay Auction page (source eBay)

In a similar vein, eBay has taken precautions to reduce cognitive strain and decision paralysis. Despite the enormous amount of products up for bid, the homepage item gallery obstinately won't grow above six pictures. The user is not given an unending list when they click "See all". Instead, a scrolling grid is used to display the auctions, with about six items being viewable at any given moment.

The divisions on individual auction pages are delineated by gray lines:

- A left-side vertical image gallery portion
- A related piece is the bottom carousel chunk.
- With portions of a product description in the middle
- On the right, a vendor information section

This chunking is essential for page skimming and navigation.

In conclusion, Miller's Law is a useful principle for information design and interpretation across a range of disciplines. Professionals may design more efficient, interesting, and user-friendly experiences while reducing cognitive overload by knowing and respecting the cognitive constraints of the human mind.

JAKOB'S LAW AND FAMILIARITY IN DESIGN

Humans are sophisticated beings. Despite having a curious and exploratory disposition, we find enormous comfort in routine. Consistency is one of the most crucial aspects of usability design since we like to predict our future experiences based on our prior ones. A single design language fosters uniformity and societal understanding, much like any other language. Contrary to previous design languages that have existed for eons, the development of web design has necessitated the use of a standard language that has been developing since 1984. Since then, the web has expanded quickly and assimilated into our daily lives.

Key Tenets of Jakob's Law:

1. Users' Exposure to Current Products Users do spend the majority of their time on other websites or digital platforms, according to Jakob's Law. They thus establish expectations based on their overall usage of these networks.

2. Transfer of Expectations: Users frequently transfer the expectations they've developed for one

well-known product to another that at first glance seems to be comparable. Users' perceptions of and interactions with new interfaces are significantly influenced by this transfer of expectations.

3. Leveraging Mental Models: Designers can produce better user experiences by utilizing the mental models that users have already built as a result of their interactions with other platforms. Users don't have to spend mental energy learning new models; they may instead concentrate on their activities.

4. Jakob's Law suggests reducing disagreement while making modifications to an already-existing product, such as a website or app. To make the transition easier and decrease user annoyance, let consumers to stick with a previous version for a little period of time.

Jakob's Law.

Jakob's Law is a rule that nature created. It involves using a language that adheres to the well-known web principles and conventions. The "king of usability" and human-computer interaction researcher Jakob Nielsen, who introduced it, is responsible. He and colleague usability expert Donald Norman co-founded the renowned usability consulting firm Nielsen Norman Group after their research garnered public attention.Users spend the majority of their time on websites other than your website, according to Jakob's Law of the internet user experience. This indicates that visitors desire your website to operate similarly to every other website they are already familiar with. Design with user-friendly patterns in mind.

Users will project expectations from one familiar thing to another based on prior encounters. Your clients may become bewildered and confused if you experiment with anything novel and unique on your website. By making use of pre-existing mental models, we may design user interfaces that let users concentrate on their objectives rather than having to acquire new models. Applying a single, user-friendly design language will reduce disagreement.

How do mental models work?

We anticipate specific behaviors from the environment and its constituent parts. A mental model is a way of thinking and believing that there is a shared understanding of how things are intended to operate. Anything that fits with the mental model we have of the world makes us feel secure and at ease. Mental models follow the same rules as the natural law. Utilizing a consistent design language is crucial because if you break them, your audience might not forgive you.

What is a common design language?

Designing for the patterns and conventions that people are already familiar to is referred to as using a common design language. These patterns and standards are prevalent everywhere, not just online. Let's look at a real-world example to put this in perspective.

Jakob's Law illustration

You must be aware of how traffic signals operate. Stop at a red light. Go when the light is green. What if one city decides to change the course of events? Today, a red light indicates a direction change, while a green light indicates a stop. You can probably imagine that this would result in a great deal of uncertainty, annoyance, and in this instance, danger. Another illustration is the recall of nearly 1 million Jeep, Dodge, and Chrysler cars in 2016 because they departed from a standard design language. When GM altered the way some vehicles' shifting mechanisms functioned, the new design was "not intuitive and provided poor tactile and visual feedback, resulting in a clear safety issue that led to hundreds of crashes," according to the manufacturer.

There isn't a straightforward list of dos and don'ts when it comes to implementing Jakob's Law to websites and apps. The ideal way to utilize Jakob's Law will change depending on your particular sector, target market, and business.

An online example of Jakob's Law in action

E-commerce websites and applications may effectively keep users focused on the crucial tasks of locating and buying things by utilizing well-known patterns and conventions. Users' experiences will be better if the process complies with their expectations.

Online customers anticipate the following when shopping:

- On the left is a logo that reads, "I know I'm at the right store."
- The search field is in the center and is labeled "The Easiest Way to Find What I'm Looking For."
- To the right is where you log into your account; doing so helps speed up the checkout process.
- The shopping basket is located to the right ("The quickest way to checkout.")

- Additionally, users no longer require a cart as the store gets smaller or more customized—just a bag. Otherwise, the same standards are applicable.

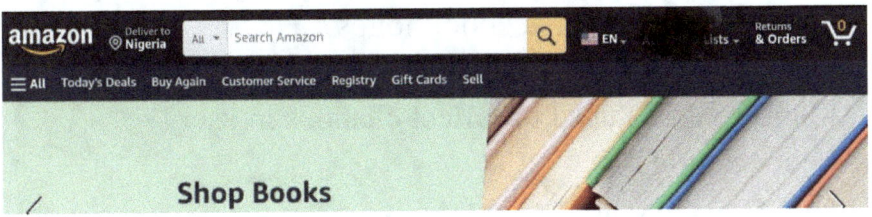

Amazon Homepage with shopping cart icon at the top right corner (source: Amazon)

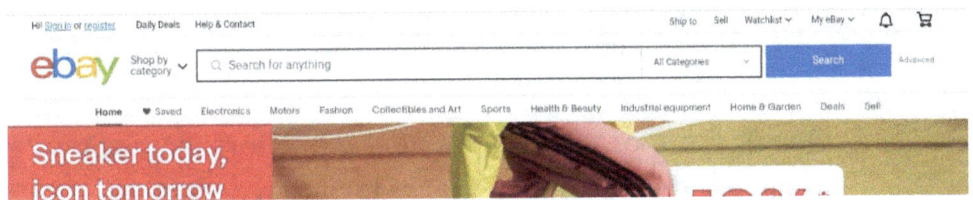

eBay Homepage with shopping cart icon at the top right corner (source: eBay)

What takes place when a website or app transgresses Jakob's Law?

Users shouldn't have to guess as to whether various expressions, circumstances, or actions have the same meaning as elsewhere. Users can access your competitors at any time by clicking away from your website or app, so they don't even need to be there. Users are hasty in their judgements and brutal in their opinions when it comes to the online. Do you still remember the new Snapchat or Facebook logos?

The six main customer experience themes below can be used to reflect changes in user expectations:

- Convenience
- Speed
- Guarantee
- Precision
- Options
- Experience

One or more of the aforementioned factors may be impacted if a design language deviation occurs. When improperly executed, too much variance can make your site more difficult to use, alienate users, and harm their interactions with your business. Occasionally, breaking off a connection entirely.

Applying Jakob's Law to your website or mobile application

All of it begins with research. The patterns and etiquette being employed in your sector are revealed by competitor research. User research reveals your customers' mental models and behavioral tendencies.

The following design facets demand careful consideration while using Jakob's Law:

- Using terminology and labeling: Using terms and explanations that your audience (and maybe not even you) will understand.
- Create visual clues for your audience's immediate use and quick understanding of the options available to them through interaction design and workflow.
- Build a content structure that can be quickly processed and simply explored by your audience using information architecture and navigation.
- Last but not least, remember to concentrate on your clients' problems rather than your own issues, preferences, or presumptions.

YouTube made a smart decision in addition to offering hilarious stuff to the world. They merely asked their users to opt-in or opt-out of new designs without making many other changes. Additionally, they routinely solicit customer input to enhance new designs. Even if you build your website or app in accordance with Jakob's Law, it won't necessarily have the same aesthetics as other websites. A digital specialist or agency has the knowledge and experience necessary to adhere to Jakob's Law of User Experience while still producing excellent work that is distinctive to your company and on-brand.

COLOR THEORY AND UX DESIGN

To create a color palette that appeals to consumers, it is essential to understand color psychology in UX design. When it comes to a design's psychological impact on consumers and, consequently, its user experience (UX), color is often overlooked by designers as a simply aesthetic option. A well-considered UX color scheme may transform a design from "good" to "great," but a subpar or poor color scheme can negatively affect a user's entire experience and even make it difficult for them to use a website or app. Although color theory in UI design is a complex topic, designers can gradually incorporate UX color best practices into their designs without having to reevaluate their entire process. The use of color in UX design encompasses much more than just creating a palette that looks nice (such as accessibility and the psychological effects of even different shades within the same hue). One of the most satisfying aspects of color theory is learning to use more unusual hues in designs once a designer has mastered the fundamentals. Barclays' website color scheme is extremely specialized.

THE PSYCHOLOGY OF COLOR

The psychology of color and the psychological effects that color may have on people are difficult and frequently arbitrary subjects. But there are some issues that can be dealt with on a larger global scale. The common meanings of the primary, secondary, and tertiary colors, conventional color schemes, and cultural differences in color meanings are all simple concepts. These fundamentals are simple for designers to grasp and include into their work. However, there are more subtleties to be discovered when it comes to the use of color in UX design. A complicated area of color theory is color psychology. It's important to consider how colors on user interfaces affect us emotionally. While some colors, like black, white, and gray, are "universal" in UX design (almost every effective design uses at least one of them), the colors they are paired with can significantly affect how a user perceives a design.

Of course, how a color is used can have a significant impact on how that color is perceived. In contrast to the same shade of blue used as an accent color in a more complicated, corporate design, blue utilized as a primary color in a modern, minimalist design will have a very different feeling.

The Emotional Triggers of Colors

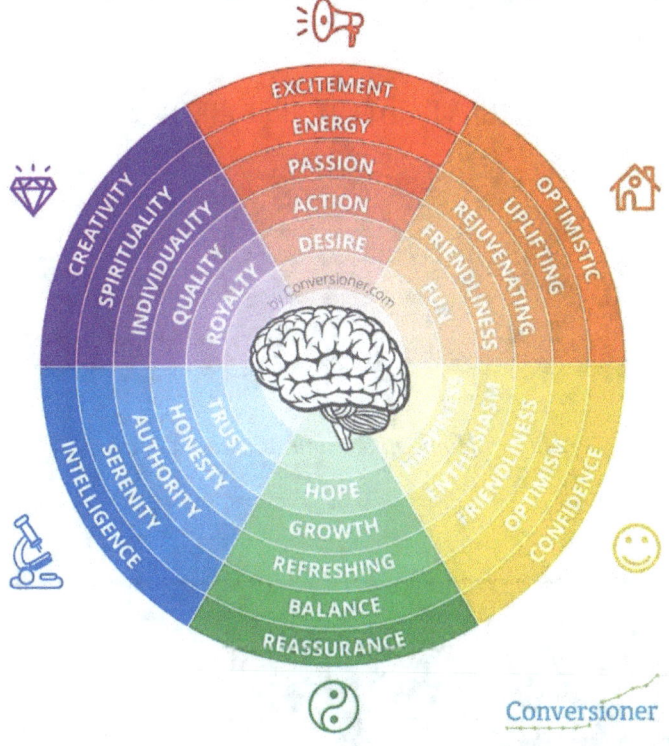

Emotional Triggers of color (source: conversioner.com)

The color palette for Zutano's website is gray and red.P&N Bank's user interface color scheme is vivid red.

Zutano Homepage (source: zutano.com)

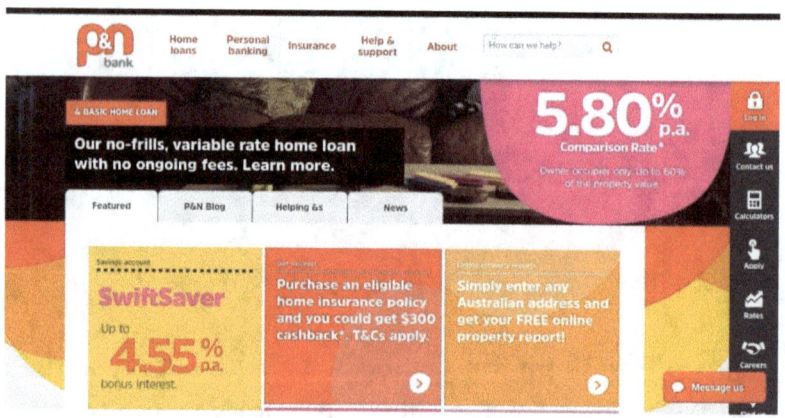

P&N Homepage (source: PN Bank.com)

COLOR DIFFERENCES BETWEEN CULTURES

The cultural variations that can surround various colors are one topic that designers frequently ignore. For instance, white is frequently linked to concepts like purity, innocence, and hope in Western societies. White, however, is connected to death, sadness, and ill karma in several parts of Asia.

Orange is a color that, regardless of country, is commonly associated with positivity, whereas white has many distinct cultural meanings around the world. When attempting to produce a design that would appeal to the broadest audience possible, this can undoubtedly complicate the designer's life. Based on the target market for the product or website, designers must consider the cultural implications of their color schemes. To avoid offensive cultural connotations, balance the colors and imagery used while marketing a product to a global audience. Designers can pay less attention to the effects the chosen color palette may have in other cultures if a product will primarily target that culture.

Global color psychology varies, largely due to cultural relationships Wanted: full-time independent UX designers living in the US. Brand values should be a major consideration when choosing a color scheme. Matching UX colors to the brand. However, they are not the only crucial element. Industry standards and colors previously employed by rivals are also important. Using a color scheme that is almost identical to that of a brand's main rival is a certain method to create confusion and guarantee that the product won't stand out. Of course, there are some exceptions. Consider Wendy's and McDonald's as examples. They are both fast food outlets that compete directly with one another. Both also employ a red and yellow color scheme. But if you compare their logos, you'll notice that McDonald's is the reverse of Wendy's, with a red background and yellow accents. Additionally distinguishing the brands, their packaging makes distinct uses of these hues. Because of this, even without logos and other distinguishing features on their packaging, neither would be easily mistaken for the other.

Unexpected UI color schemes can do a lot to distinguish a business from its rivals. Understanding the significance of the various colors and how changing their hue, saturation, brightness, or other properties might influence them is the first step in developing a brand color palette that supports the company's values. The basic definitions of the various hues are as follows:

- The color red is associated with danger, passion, and excitement. It's a really powerful color that can cause individuals to have strong reactions. Darkening the color to maroon makes it more modest and traditional, while lightening it to pink makes it more romantic and feminine.
- Orange is a very imaginative color that is also connected to youth and exploration. It's also quite spirited. Orange can also inspire a nostalgic sense because to its close ties to 1970s fashion.
- Yellow: Yellow is upbeat, positive, and cheery. It's popular in both kid and adult-friendly designs. Brighter yellows are preferred in imaginative designs, while more pastel shades are frequently utilized as a gender-neutral baby color.
- Gold, a deeper shade of yellow that represents success and wealth.
- Green: This color has many connotations. While it powerfully evokes ideas of environmentalism and nature, it also evokes sentiments of richness and tradition (especially when used in darker shades). Lime greens are frequently connected to rebirth and expansion.

- Blue — The color blue and trust are frequently linked. Blues that are more subdued and darker can be connected to sadness and depression, whereas blues that are brighter can be connected to communication. The fact that blue is the most popular color in the world may help to explain why so many businesses choose blue hues for their branding.
- Purple — Another color with a variety of connotations is purple. Since purple dye was uncommon in many ancient cultures, it was only used by royalty, hence it has a long history of being connected to monarchy and riches. But it also has a spiritual and enigmatic connotation. Purple can also inspire original thought.
- Black connotes richness and sophistication. However, it can also be connected to sadness and negativity. The other UX colors that are utilized with black can give it a modern or traditional, official or informal, vibe.
- White – White is associated with innocence, cheerfulness, and purity. Due to its simplicity and neutrality, white is a favorite color for minimalist designs. Similar to black, white readily adopts the traits of the colors it is used with.

- Gray — Depending on the context, gray can have many connotations. It could be formal and elegant or drab and dreary. It might be emotionless or irritable. It's also connected to grief and sorrow.
- Brown – Brown, which is actually a deep shade of orange, is related to earthiness and a sense of grounding. Additionally, it is connected to comfort and even nature. Of course, it can also be connected to being filthy or dingy. Designers may create color palettes for any business or product with confidence by using these fundamental color meanings as a foundation.

But color theory is a combination of science and art. A color can be seen in multiple ways even though it is typically linked to a specific emotion or mood. This can be done by combining it with other colors, changing the hue, or shifting how it is utilized in conjunction with other design components.

Enhancing UX by utilizing well-established color psychology is a good strategy. Utilizing Non-Traditional UX Colors Unusual UX color usage is a terrific method to distinguish a brand. It's also not that tough to learn how to use surprising colors in UX designs, even though it does require more skill than simply combining any old colors a designer feels like combining. The simplest place to begin when incorporating unusual colors into a design is with accent colors. A website for a legal office, for instance, would utilize the conventional color scheme of gray and navy blue. However, if you add some lime green elements, the design will stand out from the sea of other legal firms with websites that are navy blue and gray. Or take a look at this illustration from Hogan Lovells, which makes use of a modern color scheme to build a website that stands apart from other legal business websites. Compared to the average law website, it would appeal to a younger, more contemporary audience. Unexpected color palette for a website Another website with an unusual color scheme is Berdan Real Estate. The real estate website uses peach and yellow hues, both of which are far more vibrant than the typical property website (which primarily uses blue, red, and green).

On this real estate website, there is yet another unusual color palette. Although the insurance sector isn't typically thought of as cutting edge or modern, it doesn't mean their designs can't be. The color palette on Lemonade's website is gray and white with pops of fuchsia. It is totally unanticipated in a sector that isn't known for taking chances. The Lemonade website uses an unexpected UX color scheme. The web is filled with a ton of other real-world examples of unconventional UX color schemes that might be used as inspiration.

RULES 60-30-10

A straightforward approach for developing color palettes that are harmonious and visually appealing is the 60-30-10 Rule. The concept is that 60% of the color pallet is made up of one color, which is typically something rather neutral (either literally or psychologically). 30% of the color pallet is made up of a complementary color. The remaining 10% of the design is then accented with a third color. By using this technique, designers can start experimenting with unusual color schemes without deviating too far from the accepted standards within a certain industry or brand. A design that would otherwise be expected of a certain brand can be improved by adding a splash of an unexpected color. It can also be the initial step in developing a brand palette that is significantly more innovative than those of its rivals, differentiating the brand and enhancing its recall.

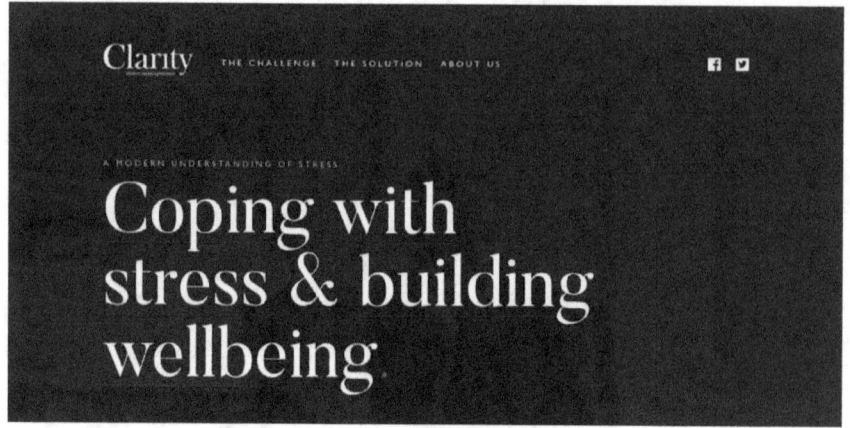

An outstanding illustration of the web design color theory's 60-30-10 rule (source:claritystressmanagement.co.uk.)

Although color theory is a hard subject, learning the fundamentals isn't extremely challenging. Designers can then expand on their skills to produce more intricate and diverse color palettes for their projects.

A well-designed color scheme is more than just a matter of taste, especially if it contains some surprising tones. Users may experience substantial psychological affects from it, and UX designers should take use of these effects to produce more effective experiences.

TYPOGRAPHY AND READABILITY

Typography is a vital component of design that directly affects readability and user experience; it goes beyond choosing fonts and positioning text. Making material readable, accessible, and interesting requires striking the proper balance of fonts, sizes, space, and formatting. We'll talk about the connection between design readability and typography in this topic. Is also a branch of graphic design that use typefaces and their arrangement to provide interfaces or experiences that are readable, accessible, and ideally, user-friendly. Effective typography improves user experience, maximizes usability, grabs users' attention, and may boost conversion rates. In order to clear up any misunderstandings regarding typographic vocabulary, we've put together the list of terms below. Although not a complete list, this particular group of phrases is especially pertinent to you as a UX designer.

The success of a website or app can be determined by its typography. More than 90% of the information available online is in text form; it's a tenet of UX design. But choosing a stylish font for your website or app is just the beginning of the typography design discipline. Several factors need to be taken into account when using typography. Here is a glossary of words and a collection of typography guidelines to assist you learn more about this field and develop user-friendly designs.

TYPOGRAPHY TERMS

Typeface: The term "typeface" refers to the faces of actual letter blocks and is also used to describe a font family. Similar to how an album is made up of tracks or a book of chapters, a typeface is made up of fonts. A typeface has different font weights, and all letters, numbers, and symbols use the same design. Typefaces include Arial, Times New Roman, and yes, even Comic Sans.

Typefaces of Sans-serif, Script, space, stencil, typewriter etc.

Font: Within a typeface, fonts are distinct weights. You select a typeface and employ a font. Georgia bold, Georgia italic, and Georgia regular are the fonts you would choose if you decided to use Georgia as your typeface. In other words, a font is a typeface's distinctive, stylized qualities. You'll probably employ two or three fonts for each project, and they'll serve as the basis for your typography and a crucial component of your entire aesthetic.

Character: is a distinct component, most often consisting of a single letter, number, or punctuation mark.

Baseline: The invisible dividing line between each letter. To create a unified layout, you can make a grid utilizing the baseline of your chosen type. Learn more about grid systems by clicking here.

X-height: The space between the baseline and the height of the lowercase letter "x" is known as the "x-height." When using a typeface with an exceptionally large (or tiny) x-height, the entire interface may be affected, occasionally even the layout.

Stroke: A stroke is a single, curved, or angled line that forms the majority of a letter.

Serif: the connecting stroke, or foot-like feature, at the end of some typefaces' principal strokes.

Because the tiny "feet" help readers' eyes move to the next character, serif typefaces are frequently easier to read. But because of their small size, they might not always display effectively on displays.

Sans Serif: A typeface without strokes or any additional details at the bottom of a letter is known as sans serif. Because displays have lower resolutions, sans serifs are frequently chosen for digital interfaces. This may no longer be a deciding factor in selecting a typeface as technology advances and screens are outfitted with higher resolutions.

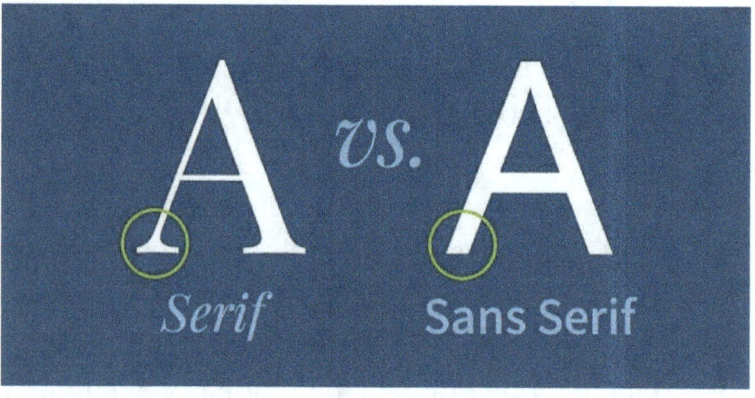

Difference between Serif and Sans Serif (source: Clockwork design group, Inc)

Weight, height, and size: These three terms describe the width, height, and size of a typeface. You can experiment with various font weights and sizes and selectively use the variations to your interface to break up the monotony of lengthy text passages or to draw attention to particular areas.

Ascender and descender: The vertical stroke that continues either upward past the x-height or downward past the baseline is known as an ascender or descender.

Letter spacing (or tracking): is the space between each character's widest point. The regular increase or decrease in the horizontal distance between characters is known as tracking.

White space: The space between elements in a design composition is referred to as "white space," sometimes known as "negative space." It will be difficult to understand the copy if the white space is not balanced.

Alignment: The term "alignment" describes the placement of text. The four primary alignments are justified, centered, left, and right. Alignment aids in the building of a logical whole by designers.

Hierarchy: The concept of organizing components in a hierarchy based on relevance. Helping users decide where to look first requires building a solid hierarchy. No matter the size of the screen, if an interface contains several pieces, it is crucial to direct the user to the screen's most crucial components. This hierarchy is created through the combination of your chosen font's weight, size, letter spacing, alignment, and surrounding white space with other visual design aspects.

TYPOGRAPHY FUNDAMENTALS

The following typography standards will help you create a website or app that is as user-friendly as possible. Although by no means comprehensive, this list offers a solid foundation for your developing typography practice.

1. An excessive number of typefaces impairs user experience

Ensure simplicity! Confusion and messy visuals can result from using too many typefaces. It's preferable to limit your typeface selection in design to two to three. Additionally increasing the size and loading time of applications is the use of different typefaces. Use typefaces that are likely to be installed or available on the users' end to improve the user experience.

2. Select typefaces that contrast and complement one another.

If your typefaces are too similar, the subtleties of each one will be missed. Selecting a serif and a sans serif font will help you create contrast.

3. Prioritize readability, legibility, and accessibility.

If your typography produces text that is difficult to understand, it will be useless for conveying information through text. Think about your consumer, their surroundings, and the media they're using to interact with your product. Accessibility can be made or broken by color and contrast; for example, pale yellow lettering on an orange backdrop will be harder to read than the same yellow type on a navy background. The popularity of "dark mode" is a good way to demonstrate the significance of accessibility because it lessens eye strain caused by bright screens while also enhancing overall readability and legibility (your text is easy to follow, overly-complicated words are avoided, and overwrought sentence structures are avoided). According to several studies, serifs are less accessible than sans-serifs, especially for users who are dyslexic. But the research comes up empty. Always test your designs with actual users to ensure that they are accessible.

4. Outstanding visual hierarchy enhances UX

Your app's or website's type hierarchy is essential since it enables visitors to browse through information quickly. Prioritize your material by making the most crucial elements the most noticeable and the least crucial elements the smallest and least intrusive. Visual hierarchy can be effectively created using size, weight, and color. When constructing a page, start with a and place the subsequent type styles beneath, from, and beyond. An added benefit of a strong hierarchy is that it boosts SEO.

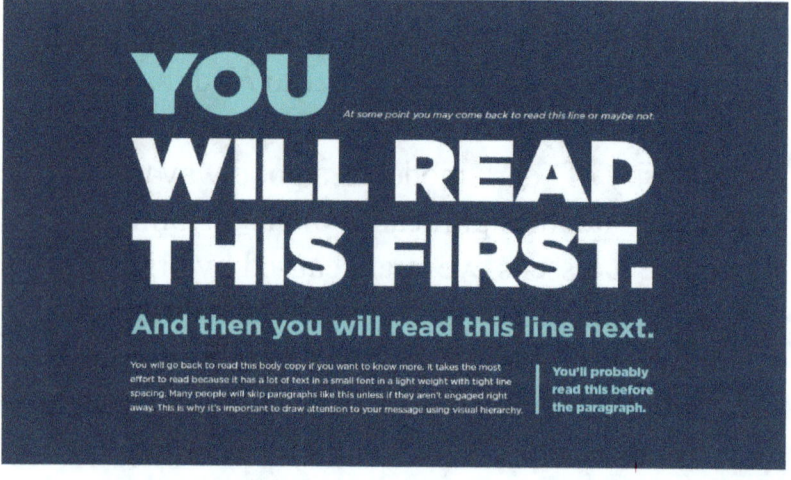

Perfect example of visual hierarchy in UX (source: Chaosamran_Studio)

5. Scale up your typography

You'll be required to construct a website or app that functions on both desktop and mobile platforms. Therefore, it's crucial to design your font with the user's experience on both platforms in mind. No matter the size of the screen, your typography should scale effectively. Set a scale at the outset of the design process for your font and typefaces. Keep in mind that your scaling rules should account for various platforms and operating systems.

6. Enrich UX with typography

The total visual language you use to communicate with your users includes typography. Typography can convey a product in the way you want it perceived, just like the visual elements of color, form, and pattern can.

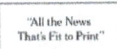

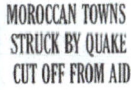

The New York Times uses calligraphy for its logo and a serif font for its headlines, evoking a classic, hard copy newspaper

(source: New York Times)

Although typography sometimes appears to be a subtle aspect of design, it is essential to producing a satisfying user experience. Understanding the fundamental concepts and rules of typography will improve the effectiveness of your designs. Don't overcomplicate your life (or design) by trying to do too much with type; simplicity is your friend. Your typeface should ultimately be intelligible, accessible, and understandable. Words matter, but so does how they seem. Therefore, the user experience will be enhanced if your typography is better.

MOBILE-FIRST DESIGN

Mobile-First Design is a seamless and streamlined experience for consumers accessing material on mobile devices is prioritized in mobile-first design, a user-centric approach to web and app design. Adopting a mobile-first strategy is crucial for reaching a large and diversified audience due to the ever-increasing use of smartphones and tablets. The goal of "Mobile-First Design" is to give smartphone users the best possible user experience (UX). Web designers and developers can contribute to a seamless user experience for visitors using smartphones and tablets by creating a website that prioritizes these people.Instead than starting with a desktop design and attempting to adapt it to mobile devices, a mobile-first design starts by designing a website or application that is optimized for mobile devices and then scaling it up to larger screens.Designing for mobile first makes sure that users on smaller displays enjoy a seamless and intuitive experience because mobile devices have taken over as the main way that people access the internet. For a mobile-first design strategy to be successfully implemented, working with the top IT service providers can be essential.In order to make a website or application seem nice on any screen size, responsive design approaches are frequently used, the layout is usually simplified, and emphasis is placed on the most crucial functions and information.

Advantages of mobile-first design include:

1. Enhancing the user experience By giving mobile users priority, interfaces may be made to be more efficient and intuitive, improving the user experience as a whole. This strategy encourages designers to streamline content and navigation, resulting in designs that are more aesthetically pleasing and user-friendly.

2. Faster Load Times: Mobile-First Design promotes asset optimization for mobile networks to enable faster asset loading, which benefits consumers on slower connections and lowers bounce rates.

3. Improved SEO Mobile-friendly websites perform better in search results on search engines like Google. The exposure and search engine rankings of your website can be increased with mobile-first design.

4. Cost effectiveness: By planning for mobile devices upfront, you can avoid later, expensive retrofitting or rebuilding to accommodate smaller screens.

5. Accessibility: For users with disabilities who depend on screen readers or other assistive technology, prioritizing mobile design frequently results in cleaner, more accessible user interfaces.

FACTORS FOR MOBILE-FIRST WEB DESIGN

- Put your users first in your design
- Create a visual hierarchy for your content
- keep your website simple.
- Make CTAs and other elements mobile-first. Continuously and Clearly
- Improve the Speed of Your Website

Even if you have appealing and data-driven advertising approaches, people who use your website or app on mobile and have a bad UX are 62% less likely to make a purchase from you in the future. That distinction is made through a website that is well-designed.

Follow these mobile-first design best practices to enhance the quality of your mobile-first website and prevent poor design from driving away customers:

1. Put Your Users at the Center of Your Design Research and determining the problems that your users have are the first steps in creating mobile-first designs. A mobile-first website should make it easier for users to carry out tasks or find solutions fast. Choose the user journeys and flows you want to use on your mobile-first website. On each website page, take into account various user behavior scenarios and modify your user's journey accordingly.

Consider the interactions that may occur between a user and the website interface in order to improve the usability and intuitiveness of your website.

You can do this by:

- Investigating and evaluating the mobile-friendly solutions of your rivals
- Using surveys to directly ask your visitors about the difficulties they are having with your mobile website

2. Create a Visual Hierarchy for Your Content
The content on a website designed with mobile users in mind should be as brief and direct as feasible. Avoid filler, clutter, and any other extraneous stuff that could confuse, overwhelm, or distract readers or make the content difficult to read.Due to the screen size limitations of mobile websites, it is important to respect the visual hierarchy of content value when presenting content to your audience. You'll be able to tell which components are most crucial and have to come first.The enhancement of content facilitates UX and increases website performance. It also improves accessibility and ADA compliance for the website.

Follow these best practices while creating mobile-first content and arranging it hierarchically:

- To ensure that readers can see and understand the material right away, keep article titles at the top and article previews above the fold.
- For flawless performance on mobile devices, optimize the sizes of your images and videos.
- Keep your content succinct and concise.
- Break up large paragraphs into numerous, easily skimmed one-sentence pieces.

It can be difficult to create aesthetically appealing and meaningful material, especially if content marketing is not your area of expertise. To create strategic content for each digital channel and stage of your online conversion funnel, if you need assistance, get in touch with top content marketing services.

3. Keep It Simple On Your Website: Improved content clarity and user attention are two benefits of simple and minimalist web design. Keep the most crucial components and get rid of the rest when creating a website that is optimized for mobile. Use of intrusive and off-putting components, such as pop-ups and advertisements, should be avoided.

Consider these steps when trying to make your website more user-friendly for mobile users:

- Count the links on your navigation menu less frequently.
- Don't make it too small for mobile displays; use plain fonts.
- Utilize broad boundaries and crisp lines.
- Use as few pages as feasible on your website.
- Include a useful search engine function.

- To make the layout more readable and less crowded, use white space.
- Use no more than two columns of content.

4. Create CTAs and other content that is mobile-first regular and Bold: For websites that are mobile-friendly, simple shapes, vivid colors, and typography are fantastic. A mobile-first requirement is to include these components into a compelling call-to-action (CTA) button. Use these striking CTAs instead of links, which can be challenging to tap on mobile displays.

Other visually appealing mobile-first components that improve UX and direct customers through the sales funnel should be appealing. These consist of:

- Readability of the navigation buttons
- Vibrant hues and contrasting color combinations
- Abstract designs and geometric forms
- Backgrounds with images or videos and parallax scrolling
- Add a touch of individualization with hand-drawn graphics
- Amazing typography

5. Improve the Site's Loading Time: According to research, if a website takes

longer than three seconds to fully load, visitors will leave. On mobile devices, loading time is equally crucial because it influences user experience and search engine rankings. For this reason, you should remove extraneous content from mobile-first websites.

Following these protocols will increase your speed:

- Your photos should be compressed to "lose weight" while maintaining quality.
- Use "lazy load," which loads website pieces sequentially and independently so that consumers can see some portions of your website right away.
- Change to the secure HTTPS protocol, which is quicker and improves SEO.
- Use a CDN that pulls content from the cache closest to the user to load the website.

MOBILE INTERACTION AND PATTERN

In order to give users seamless and interesting experiences, it is essential to develop successful mobile interactions. Mobile devices have become an essential part of our daily lives. Interaction patterns for mobile devices are well-established design methods that handle typical user chores and difficulties on small screens. They aid in ensuring the uniformity, effectiveness, and usability of mobile app and website design. The following list of significant mobile interaction patterns includes:

1. Navigational Patterns

   - Hamburger selections: The hamburger menu, symbolized by three horizontal lines, is a typical design for condensing navigation options. When the icon is touched, a menu with links to the app's many sections or functions appears.

   - Tab Bar: Typically found at the bottom of the screen, tab bars provide easy access to the main views or parts of an app. They are particularly common in the design of iOS apps.

   - Drawer Navigation The drawer navigation pattern slides out a panel from the side of the screen to offer navigation options, much like the hamburger menu. It is frequently applied to Android app design.

2. Hand gestures

    -   Swipe: Users can scroll horizontally over content or switch between pages or photos by using swipe movements. Swiping can also make things being deleted or archived.

    -   Pinch and Zoom:Users can zoom in and out of images or content using pinch-to-zoom movements, which makes it simpler to see details on small screens.

3. Form Entry Patterns:

    -   Forms with a single column: To guarantee that every input field is immediately visible and accessible while minimizing the need for horizontal scrolling, forms are often provided in a single-column layout for mobile devices.

    -   Numerical Keypad Mobile devices frequently transition to a numeric keypad layout for numeric input, which makes it quicker and more natural for users to enter numbers.

- "Autocomplete and Suggestions" Autocomplete and recommendation patterns are frequently used in mobile apps to speed up and improve form field completion.

4. Skewing Patterns:

   - Infinite scrolling Apps and social media feeds frequently employ infinite scroll to load new material as users scroll down. It offers a fluid and interesting browsing experience.

   - Parallax scrolling When visitors scroll, background components are moved at a different speed from the foreground text, adding depth and visual intrigue.

5. Organization of the content

   - Menus in an accordion Users can expand and compress content sections to conserve space while still having access to in-depth information using accordion menus.

- Sliders and Carousels: Sliders and carousels are useful for displaying a number of articles or photos in a small area.

6. Recommendations and Alerts:

- Toast notifications include: Toast notifications are discreet pop-up messages that inform users of feedback or alerts without interfering with what they are doing right now.

- Banner notifications include: Users are alerted to significant events or updates with the quick appearance of banner notifications at the top or bottom of the screen.

7. Navigation Hand gestures:

- Swipe to navigate: Users can browse backwards or forwards within an app or website by swiping from the edge of the screen, which provides a practical way to switch between pages.

- Double tapping: When you double-tap a screen element, you can zoom in or out, start an action, or get more details.

8. Targets for Touch and Interactions:

- "Finger Friendly Touch Targets" Users can accurately interact with touch targets (buttons, icons, and links) using their fingers if they are designed with adequate size and spacing.

- Long Press: For elements in a list or grid, long-press interactions can display extra options or context menus.

Effective mobile interaction patterns accommodate the limitations and capabilities of small screens to improve the user experience. The patterns that best serve the objectives of an app or website should be carefully chosen by the designer, who should then adapt the patterns to the demands of the user while preserving consistency and usability throughout the interface. To consistently enhance the mobile user experience, it is also crucial to keep up with new trends and technology in mobile engagement.

RESPONSIVE DESIGN AND PRINCIPLES

Mobile devices are being accommodated by desktop websites using responsive web design. Smaller screens are scaled down after the desktop version. Although tailored for "classic" desktop websites, the content, navigation, and layout are shrunk to accommodate the mobile devices. Designing for mobile devices first is more akin to creating a mobile app and changing the layout for desktop computers while keeping the qualities of a great user experience, such quick download times and streamlined content to interest the audience. Working with a reputable mobile app development company will help you make sure that your design is user-friendly and appropriate for mobile platforms. The content of websites is automatically adjusted via responsive web design so that users may read it easily on a variety of screens. The mobile-first approach, which starts from the more constrained mobile end and strives to increase features for the desktop, puts the needs of mobile users first.

The goal of responsive design is to maximize adaptation across a range of devices and screen sizes. Whether customers browse your site on a desktop computer, tablet, smartphone, or other device, it makes sure that your content and user interface elements automatically adjust to deliver an optimal experience. Take into account these fundamental ideas to develop responsive design successfully:

1. Fluid Grid Layout:

- Percentage-Based Layouts: Instead of using fixed pixel values to specify the widths and heights of items, use relative units like percentages. This enables material to adjust adaptably to various screen sizes.

- Media questions: To apply different styles dependent on screen width, use media queries in CSS. This gives you the option to modify the design elements for different screen sizes, including the layout and text sizes.

2. Images and media that are adaptable:

- Image Scaling: Make sure that images scale proportionally to fit various screen widths by using CSS to ensure that distortion is avoided.

- Responsive Media Embeds Use the responsive embed codes offered by websites like YouTube or Vimeo for videos and other embedded material. These scripts modify media files to fit different screen widths.

3. A mobile-first strategy

- Design for Mobile Devices First: Start creating with mobile devices in mind. Make a layout that is practical and user-friendly for tiny screens, then gradually improve it for larger screens.

- Content Priority: Give critical content top priority for mobile users to make sure they can quickly access the most crucial information.

4. Breakpoints and media inquiries:

- Strategic Turning Points Create breakpoints at important screen widths where design modifications are required. Breakpoints for PCs, tablets, and smartphones are typical.

- Planning for Media Query:Consider carefully how content and design components should change at various screen sizes when planning your media queries. To achieve a seamless transition between breakpoints, conduct extensive testing.

5. Readability and Typography:

- "Responsive Fonts" To ensure readability on diverse displays, use relative units for font sizes, such as ems or percentages.

- Line Length Keep your lines between 50 and 75 characters long to improve readability on all devices.

6. Touch and Tap Optimization.

- Touch-Friendly Components Make sure touchscreen devices can easily tap interactive elements like buttons and links by making sure they are big enough.

- Spacing:To reduce inadvertent taps and enhance user experience, create enough padding and space between interactive items.

7. Test results and user comments:

- Testing across devices: Test your design frequently on different platforms and browsers to find and fix responsive bugs.

- User Feedback: Collect comments from users on various devices to learn about their experiences and adjust the product as necessary.

8. Performance improvement:

- Loading Speed: Make sure that materials like photos and scripts load quickly, especially on sluggish mobile connections.

- Conditional loading: To improve performance, conditionally load resources based on screen sizes and device capabilities.

2. Accessibility

- Accessible Design: Make sure users with impairments can access your responsive design. Check for compatibility with screen readers and offer alternative text for photos.

3. Content Versatility

- Content Priority: Select the content that must always be visible and that can be concealed on smaller displays by menus or accordions.

A seamless and accessible user experience across a variety of devices depends on responsive design concepts. Designers should make sure that their websites and apps stay relevant and user-friendly in an increasingly diversified digital ecosystem by adhering to these principles and keeping up with changing technologies and user preferences.

3 TOP EXAMPLES OF MOBILE-FIRST WEBSITES

1. La Teva Website

Mobile Design for La Teva Website

La Teva Web, a web design company, has a mobile-first website that complies with the majority of PWA best practices since it eliminates application caching and requests the geolocation permission only when the page is loaded. This website is very user-friendly, and the material is proportioned suitably for the viewport and tap targets. The website makes advantage of progressive JPEGs to enhance performance.

Primary mobile-first components:
- Logical navigation
- Brief contact form
- Sliding content
- Responsive typography

2. International Energy Agency.

Mobile Design for International Energy Agency Website

The user profile, search, and menu are all neatly tucked away at the top of this mobile-first website along with the brand's emblem, opening and showcasing their capabilities with a single tap. This website features a lot of blog posts, thus a single column layout that encourages readers to scroll down for additional content improves usability. A large headline is displayed to visitors alongside beautiful photos, along with a CTA link that opens the content.

Primary mobile-first components:

- A hamburger menu with easily accessible extra content
- Good-quality photographs that are efficiently compressed for a fast website
- Large headlines with brief introductions
- One-column design

3. Festa da Francofonia.

Mobile Design forFesta da Francofonia

One of the best instances of mobile-first site design is Festa de Francofonia. This website for the events sector encourages content revisions and uses notification strategies. It uses the HTTPS protocol, which considerably improves its speed by diverting HTTP traffic to it. For the best mobile speed, it also uses file compression and minifies CSS, HTML, and JavaScript. This website meets the needs of users of portable devices thanks to the use of legible font sizes, color contrasts, and the prioritizing of visible material in terms of user experience.

Primary mobile-first components:

- Geometric style
- An extremely basic menu
- Quickly loading
- Specific animation

Less writing, large fonts, eye-catching CTAs, quick loading times, and optimized video and image content are all part of mobile-first web design's goal to provide a complete mobile UX. As mobile technology develops, smartphone devices and their browsers will make greater use of capabilities like cameras, speech recognition, and haptic feedback. As a result, the mobile-first strategy will be in charge of delivering the best user experience. Businesses that employ it will continue to outperform their rivals in bringing in relevant visitors and producing leads. Top web design companies can assist you in developing a mobile-first design strategy and building a website that is suited to the requirements of your audience if you need assistance with making your website more mobile-friendly.

USER RESEARCH AND USABILITY TESTING

User research and usability testing are essential steps in the creation of new products. They offer priceless information about user behavior, preferences, and problems, ultimately assisting in the development of user-focused, efficient, and interesting products. The secret to any business' success is gathering user feedback, whether you're launching an app, rebuilding a website, enhancing a product feature, or continuously improving your client experience.User research and usability testing are approaches used to understand users' actions and are frequently used interchangeably. User research is a subfield of usability testing. Let's examine usability testing and user research topics, their significance, and how they help to enhance the user experience:

USER RESEARCH

User research is a methodical way to comprehending the preferences, wants, and motivations of the target market for a good or service. It is crucial in determining user-centered design and making sure that products successfully satisfy customer expectations. The term "user research" serves as a catch-all for various types of user testing, including usability testing, questionnaires, and interviews. Overall, user research puts customers at the center of your design process, helps you develop your products, and reveals user insights. It is the process of examining user interactions to support the creation of experiences and products that put people first.

USER RESEARCH TYPES

There are several user research techniques available that produce useful information. Depending on your needs, there are numerous ways to do user research. There are a number of techniques available if you want to learn about user behavior, comprehend user preferences, or simply concentrate on becoming more customer-centric. Here are some.

QUALITATIVE VS. QUANTITATIVE RESEARCH

You could be unsure of whether to utilize a qualitative or quantitative UX research strategy when trying to understand your users. Finding that out is crucial because the two types produce quite different findings.

You need to know both what is happening and why in order to fully comprehend your user experience. If you simply have quantitative data, you can be overlooking crucial insights that could alter how well you comprehend the user experience. Additionally, you won't be able to determine whether your findings are representative of a larger population if you simply conduct qualitative research.

ATTITUDINAL VS. BEHAVIORAL RESEARCH

Attitude and behavioral studies are not the same, although occasionally being confused as such. However, when compared side by side, the two can be helpful, just as with quantitative and qualitative research. Assessment of users' preexisting attitudes or thoughts toward an experience is a component of attitude research. For instance, you might do this by first asking a user why they favor or dislike a feature on your website. Comparatively, behavioral research focuses on user behavior.

Another analogy to the gap between quantitative and qualitative methodologies is that while attitudinal research serves to explain why something is happening, behavioral research helps to explain what is happening. Always remember that users' statements and actions frequently diverge.

GENERATIVE VS EVALUATION RESEARCH

Research that is both generative and evaluation-focused (also known as evaluative research) has quite diverse objectives. You can better describe the issue you want to create a solution for with the aid of generative research. On the other hand, evaluation research aids in the evaluation of an existing design (whether it be in prototype, final, or another form).

Here is a detailed evaluation of user research, its techniques, and the reasons why it is important in the design and development process:

Key User Research Elements

1. Customer Personas: Developing fictionalized versions of typical users is a step in the process of creating detailed user personas. These personas aid teams in understanding and designing for particular user segments.

2. User Interviews: Individual interviews with users offer qualitative information about their experiences, problems, objectives, and preferences. Design choices are informed by these observations.

4. Surveys and Questionnaires: Surveys gather quantitative information from a bigger user base to spot patterns and trends in user behavior, demographics, and opinions.

5. Contextual Inquiry: Researchers spend time in consumers' contexts to study how they utilize tools, services, or goods. This approach offers detailed contextual insights.

6. Competitive Analysis: Researching the products of rival companies can help you find industry norms, best practices, and potential for distinction.

7. A/B Testing: "A/B tests" compare two iterations of a feature or product to see which one performs better in terms of user engagement and satisfaction.

8. Heat maps and analytics: Data about user activity is available through web and app analytics, including page visits, click-

through rates, and session length. Heatmaps show the locations of user interaction and clicks.

The User Research Methodology

1. Define the following goals: Start by outlining your research's goals, including what you hope to learn, your target market, and the size of your study.

2. Find Participants: Find individuals who fit the desired user profile and recruit them. Think about your psychographics, behaviors, and demographics.

3. Data Gathering: Utilize a variety of research techniques, such as observations, surveys, or interviews, to collect pertinent information from participants.

4. Evaluation: To glean insights that can be put to use, carefully assess the information gathered. Determine trends, trouble spots, and areas that may be improved.

5. Create user personas, journey maps, or empathy maps to assist teams comprehend and empathize with users based on the findings.

6. Make educated suggestions for design modifications, feature enhancements, or new product directions in light of the research.

The value of user research is as follows:

1. User-Centered Design: User research makes sure that design choices are based on user wants and preferences, resulting in products that have a higher chance of being successful on the market.

2. Decreases Risk: Organizations can lower the risk of investing in products or designs that don't appeal to users by understanding user behaviors and motivations.

3. Innovation: User research frequently identifies unmet requirements and chances for innovation, assisting in the creation of new goods or services.

4. Usability Improvement: It aids in discovering usability problems and pain areas, resulting in designs that are more logical and user-friendly.

5. Enhanced User Satisfaction: Consumers are more likely to be satisfied and devoted to a product when it is guided by user research.

6. Effective Marketing: User research can help firms adjust their outreach and messaging to particular user segments.

7. Cost savings: It is less expensive to address user demands and problems early in the design process than it is to make significant changes after a product has been released.

User research is a continuous process that needs to be included in the process of creating new products. Making design decisions based on data-driven insights and often asking people for input results in more successful and user-friendly products.

USABILITY TESTING

Usability testing is a user research technique used to assess a product's user interface's efficacy, efficiency, and satisfaction. In order to spot usability concerns, receive input, and make wise design choices, this technique entails watching actual consumers as they engage with a product.

Usability testing is a type of qualitative study that looks at how well an application, piece of software, or prototype works for users. By using usability testing, you may find any problems with the user experience of your product and fix them before releasing the final version, saving money and time and ensuring a well-designed final product.

Why would businesses prioritize user testing over different kinds of user research?

It is preferable to employ qualitative research over quantitative research to develop a deeper understanding of your customer. User testing is the way to go if your company wants rich, deeper information. User testing offers rich qualitative information on the opinions of your users. You get the chance to see, hear, and directly communicate with your users during user testing, whether it be through user interviews or user observation, to better understand how they feel about your product. This improves your comprehension of your target user, which in turn helps you create better goods that satisfy the needs and desires of your clients.

Usability testing and user research are complementary processes.

As you probably inferred, all types of user research are essential when businesses want to create goods that cater to their customers. You should keep an eye on how users are interacting with and responding to these new products when doing user research. This generates suggestions on how to keep improving your product. The greatest method to stay on top of consumer concerns and expectations is to often solicit feedback and ideas from your customers. By doing this, you can be sure that you're making the best choices and taking the necessary actions to maintain the loyalty and pleasure of your customers.

Here is a thorough evaluation of usability testing, its advantages, and how to do it well:

Key elements of usability testing include:

1. Participants who are users: Choose a representative sample of the target market whose members will utilize the product during the testing period. Diverse user demographics guarantee thorough feedback.

2. Tasks and Case Studies: Define the precise actions or situations consumers should take

while utilizing the product. The tasks should reflect actual use cases.

3. Moderator During the usability test, a skilled moderator leads participants while giving instructions and facilitating the procedure with the least amount of disruption possible.

4. Observation: Participants and designers keep an eye on how customers use the product. They make notes, observe user activity, and note usability problems.

5. Encourage participants to speak out as they work their way through the product using the "Think-Aloud Protocol." This makes it easier to comprehend their choices and any areas of uncertainty.

6. Recording: Usability sessions are frequently videotaped or screenshotted in order to record user interactions for further research.

The Methodology of Usability Testing

1. Planning first Define the usability test's aims, parameters, and scope. Create a test plan that details scenario development, participant recruiting, and success criteria.

2. Recruitment: Find participants who fit the desired user profile and recruit them. To get a variety of viewpoints, make sure there is age, experience, and background diversity.

3. Preparation: Set up the setting for the usability test, including the product prototype or website, the venue, and any equipment or software that may be required.

4. Moderation: Guide each participant through the planned situations during one-on-one usability sessions while encouraging them to voice their opinions.

5. Observation During usability sessions, multiple observers should watch and take notes. They should pay attention to usability problems, user mistakes, and angry or happy moments.

6. Evaluation: After all sessions are finished, examine the data to find patterns, usability problems, and areas that may be improved.

7. Recommendations include: Make suggestions for design modifications,

updates, or improvements based on the study to solve any identified usability issues.

Advantages of usability testing include:

1. Usability testing reveals usability issues and roadblocks that might not have been visible during the design phase.

2. User-Centered Design: It guarantees that the product complies with user demands, preferences, and expectations.

1. Efficiency Improvement: By streamlining interactions and procedures, usability testing helps make a product easier to use.

2. Error Reduction: Usability testing lowers the likelihood of user errors and misunderstandings by identifying and resolving usability concerns.

3. Saves Resources and Time: Making adjustments after a product has been released is more expensive than addressing usability issues early in the design process.

4. Increases User Contentment: Higher user satisfaction and retention rates are the results of a more usable product.

5. Competitive Advantage: Products with usability as a top priority frequently outperform rivals and obtain a competitive edge in the market.

Usability testing is an iterative process that needs to be included in the lifespan of a product. Regular usability testing sessions guarantee that customer input continues to develop and improve the product's usability, leading to a more successful and user-friendly end result.

ACCESSIBILITY IN UX

The goal of user experience (UX) design accessibility is to enable people with impairments to use digital goods and services. It guarantees that everyone can access and interact with digital content successfully, regardless of their skills or disabilities. Professionals in UI/UX always aim for a design that is user-centered. This means that the design needs to be developed, modified, and presented in such a way that all members of the target audience can easily interact with it and complete their duties. However, this strategy may be difficult. Only making a design interactive and responsive won't ensure its usability or accessibility. To make sure that the design is user-friendly and functions as expected, the designers must thoroughly comprehend the audience and address their unique issues.

Here, the notion of accessibility in UX design is relevant. Accessibility's main goal and inspiration is to make sure that both the design process and the final goods and services produced are user-centered. This means that in order to make consumers' life easier, their demands are constantly put first. Diversity is valued in the world of UX design, and a product can only succeed if it adheres to this criteria. The idea of equitable access and accessible designs must be promoted by any contemporary organization, including but not limited to a company that provides UI/UX design services. This is why a lot of businesses are creating their own accessibility statements to appeal to a wider demographic, especially when it comes to websites and mobile apps.

KEY ACCESSIBILITY PRINCIPLES:

Given that there are numerous issues to consider while designing for accessibility. It is crucial to consider how UI/UX designers can handle all these factors, making sure that their goods and services are inclusive, usable, and valuable. How can accessibility be made a crucial component of any UX design strategy, in other words?

The following are the fundamental tenets of accessible UX design.

- Research on users' empathy
- Inclusivity
- Navigational control
- Context

There are certain guidelines and concepts that designers can adhere to in this regard, even if there are no established criteria for include accessibility in the design of goods and services. Depending on the nature of the design and the design process, other concerns might be taken into account. When working on upcoming design projects, the following guidelines or accessible UX design concepts can be useful.

1. Empathy

Empathy is one of the fundamental tenets of the UX design process. Empathy becomes even more crucial when it comes to accessibility in design. When dealing with a product or service, UI/UX designers need to take the audience's demands into account and comprehend their problems. This entails speaking with users as well as viewing the prototypes through the eyes of the intended audience. With empathy, designers can connect with their audience and address their issues.

2. User research

Designing accessible designs requires the same user research that is crucial to design thinking. Designers must reach out to a wide spectrum of people when working on any project, taking into account persons with various physical and cognitive needs. This study aims to involve user agents in the design process and give them a chance to speak up. Designers must enter the actual world, seek out the target audience with a variety of demands, comprehend their worries, and address their issues with creative and practical solutions in order to make designs accessible.

3. Inclusivity

When working on any design project, UI/UX designers need to accept the criteria of inclusion and representation. The personas and user research for a product should be representative of the worldwide audience for which it is intended. The design procedure should also make sure that people with different physical capabilities are included in the creation of prototypes.

4. Navigational control

Controlling navigation is a key element of accessibility in UX design. This is crucial while attempting to make the web more accessible. Some consumers may find the goods and services used on web browsers or in mobile applications to be challenging. Giving users a variety of navigational options will help to give them the most control possible. For instance, if some of the users require assistive equipment, the designers must consider how that can affect their interaction and offer options to let them manage how they interact with the design.

5. Context

The context in which a design is utilized is one of the factors that takes into account the demands of all users, regardless of their physical and cognitive capabilities. Users of mobile applications, for instance, can interact with them while moving about, sitting, lying down, or even driving. The necessity to make sure the design is similarly responsive in all situations and environments adds another layer of complexity for designers. Context is one of the key determining elements for accessibility in UX design.

Here is are common factors of accessibility in UX and importance of accessibility:

Common accessibility factors include:

1. Text Alternatives: Give photos and other non-text items alternative text that explains what it is and what it contains. Users with visual impairments can better understand the context thanks to this.

2. Keyboard Navigation: Check that any interactive components, such as buttons,

forms, and menus, can be accessed and utilized solely with a keyboard. Try to limit your use of mouse-driven interactions.

3. Color and Contrast Options: To assist users with low eyesight, maintain a suitable contrast between the text and background colors. Don't let color be your only means of communication.

4. Flexible fonts and text sizes: Give users the option to change their preferred text size and font to suit their own reading preferences.

5. Transcripts and Captions: To help users with hearing difficulties, include transcripts for audio content and captions for videos.

6. Semantic HTML: To improve screen reader compatibility and navigation, use semantic HTML elements and appropriate content structure.

7. Form Accessibility: Ensure that forms have clear labeling, understandable error messages, and form validation that is compatible with screen readers.

8. Managing Your Focus: Make that the keyboard focus is managed properly for interactive items and that the focus indication is shown.

9. Testing using Assistive Technologies: Test your product frequently using assistive software, such as screen readers, to find and fix accessibility problems.

The Importance of Accessibility in User Experience:

1. Inclusivity: Accessibility guarantees inclusive digital experiences, enabling people with disabilities to take part fully in online activities such as socializing, learning, and purchasing.

2. Legal Compliance: Digital information must be accessible under numerous rules and laws, such as the Americans with Disabilities Act in the US. Legal repercussions may occur from non-compliance.

3. Market Expansion: Companies can reach a larger audience and client base by designing

with accessibility in mind, thus expanding their market reach.

4. Customer Contentment: Better user experiences are frequently the result of accessible designs, not just for people with disabilities. Everyone wins when usability is improved.

5. Brand Reputation: A company's reputation can be improved by its dedication to accessibility, which shows social responsibility.

6. Future-proofing: Considering accessibility helps to ensure that digital items continue to be useable as technology advances.

7. Ethical Design: Adopting accessibility is a moral strategy for design that puts the needs of all users first.

8. Innovation: Finding answers to accessibility issues can result in creative design ideas that help a larger spectrum of users.

It's not simply a great practice to incorporate accessibility into UX design; in many cases, it's also required by law. Accessibility-focused designers and organizations produce more egalitarian and user-friendly digital experiences for all users.

WEB CONTENT ACCESSIBILITY GUIDELINES (WCAG)

The World Wide Web Consortium (W3C) created a set of standards known as the Web Content Accessibility Guidelines (WCAG). The WCAG standard offers a framework for producing digital experiences and web content that are accessible to people with impairments. These rules are crucial for ensuring that everyone, regardless of ability, can access and interact with online information successfully and for making the web more inclusive.

The recommendations that follow can assist UX designers in producing accessible designs.

- Identify user personas.
- Adaptive design for all platforms and gadgets
- Logic-based content organization
- Design consistency.
- Use accessible fonts
- Select the proper color contrast.

- Add alternative text to media content
- Include transcriptions and subtitles
- Limit your animation.
- Be sure the anchor text has purpose.

We've provided some of the top recommendations for enhancing the accessibility of your upcoming projects. Consider these recommendations as a UX accessibility check list that is useful regardless of the project's scope. Just like every other design principle, keep in mind that there are many creative ways to apply these principles; they are not rigid rules.

1. Identify user personas.

The creation of user personas that are reflective of a varied audience is one of the most crucial accessibility recommendations for UX design. Depending on the nature of the product, several personas may be created; however, designers must be careful when choosing the final personas. It's usually a good idea to include audience members with specific needs.

2. Adaptive design for all platforms and gadgets

Designing for many platforms and devices is equally as important as designing for various audiences. The people interacting with a design in today's digital environment may be using devices with different operating systems, screen sizes, and features. The responsiveness of a design on such devices and platforms must be taken into account.

3. Logic-based content organization

The level of understandability of your material is closely correlated with its accessibility, whether it takes the shape of a website, a mobile application, or a physical product. The logical organization of the content is crucial for accessibility because of this. Making an information architecture that fully exemplifies how the content is organized and facilitates addressing the needs of the target audience is one way to accomplish this.

4. Design consistency.

There must be some amount of consistency in the good or service for a design to be helpful and accessible. This implies that the users should be able to easily navigate around the design without encountering any unpleasant shocks. Individuals with disabilities benefit from consistent designs since they are easier to understand and work better with tools and assistive technology.

5. Use accessible fonts

The general accessibility of the design can be significantly impacted by the way your written material is presented. Therefore, it is crucial to pick typefaces that are simple to read and do not pose any difficulties for those with special requirements. For the majority of the material, plain sans serif fonts should always be used. If you must use attractive fonts, use them sparingly and just for headings and title texts.

😁 Accessible	😓 Not accessible
Comic Sans: bad dad on no Illinois	Aguafina Script: bad dad on no Illinois
Verdana: bad dad on no Illinois	Uncial Antiqua: bad dad on no Illinois
Helvetica: bad dad on no Illinois	Henny Penny: bad dad on no Illinois

List of accessible fonts (source: Ramotion)

6. Select the proper color contrast
   One of the most significant and difficult responsibilities when it comes to accessibility is selecting the appropriate colors. The selection of colors is constrained by factors like branding and aesthetics. Here, designers must remember that not

everyone can easily tell apart between all the colors. Therefore, it is important to choose color contrast wisely so as not to impair the content's legibility.

7. Add alternative text to media content
   The inclusion of alt-text with all media assets is a quick and powerful technique to increase the accessibility of online content. This means that a brief descriptive text that screen readers can understand should be present with all of the photos, videos, and animations. By doing this, those who have visual impairments can also comprehend the meaning of the image and its function within the design.

8. Include subtitles and transcriptions
   Transcripts and subtitles are powerful tools for developing accessible designs in addition to alt-text. These not only assist those who suffer from hearing and vision impairments, but also meet the requirements of a worldwide audience. Here, designers can also incorporate translations into several languages, enabling a broad audience to interact with the good or service.

9. Limit your animation

It may be tempting to fill the design with a lot of moving pictures. Consideration must be given to this decision. To ensure that all users may interact with the content fairly, it is advised to mix text and visual aspects within the content. Additionally, some people may find moving visuals unsettling, especially flashing ones, therefore they should be avoided.

10. Be sure the anchor text has purpose. Make sure the anchor text is relevant when including links in the content. Long URLs in the text can be annoying for people who use screen readers. Meaningful links make the content more valuable while also enhancing its readability and accessibility. They also increase your authority.

Success Criteria for WCAG

The three degrees of conformity for the WCAG are Level A, Level AA, and Level AAA, with Level AAA being the most accessible level. The conditions for achieving each degree of accessibility are outlined in a set of guidelines and particular success criteria.

To ensure readability for people with low vision, a Level AA success criterion can, for instance, state that text content must have a minimum contrast ratio against its background. All Level A and Level AA success criteria must be satisfied in order to achieve Level AA conformity.

Benefits of WCAG include:

1. Inclusivity: WCAG encourages the design of digital experiences and information that may be used by people with a variety of disabilities, including those who have cognitive, motor, visual, or hearing impairments.

2. Legal Compliance: Adhering to WCAG criteria enables firms to abide by accessibility laws and rules, such as the European Accessibility Act in Europe and the Americans with Disabilities Act (ADA) in the United States.

3. Improved User Experience: Not just users with impairments, but all users generally benefit from accessible websites and apps' improved usability and user experiences.

4. Market Expansion: An accessible design can expand a product's potential user base, reaching a wider audience and enhancing market competitiveness.

5. Social accountability Putting accessibility first demonstrates a commitment to moral design principles and social responsibility.

For designers, developers, and organizations looking to produce digital content and experiences that are friendly and useful for everyone, WCAG is a helpful resource. We get one step closer to a more inclusive and equitable digital environment by adhering to the WCAG requirements. A design's effectiveness depends on how well it serves the intended audience. The improvement of consumers' life is a major obligation of UI/UX designers. This, however, cannot be accomplished if a product or service is designed with only a small group of users' wants in mind. The accessibility tenets guarantee that this bias is abolished, or at the very least reduced.

The advice provided in this chapter can assist you in producing better designs that are usable by a variety of users, paving the path for your professional success as a designer. When working on a design project, take a moment to consider the target audience, especially the people who are sometimes overlooked. This is the first step in making sure UX design is accessible.

MICRO-INTERACTIONS

Micro-interactions are little, frequently invisible design components that have a significant impact on the overall user experience of digital products. These minute interactions are intended to give consumers feedback, instruct them, and inspire responsiveness and joy. They can be found in a variety of user interface elements, including form fields, buttons, and animations. Micro-interactions are, as the name implies, brief moments of user interaction in a design. These are pairs of trigger-feedback events taking place on your website, app, or gadget. In reality, they are all around us in daily life.

Samples of micro-interactions include:

1. Animations for buttons A button changes color, shape, or size to provide visual feedback as users hover over or click it.

2. Form Validation: As users fill out a form, real-time validation notifications indicate whether the data is correct or needs to be changed.

3. Toggle switches: Switches that, when toggled, change their state to show whether a feature or setting is on or off.

4. Progress indicators that inform users that an action is ongoing, such as loading spinners, progress bars, or animations.

5. Hover Effects :refers to components that, when a user hovers over them, change appearance and provide oblique visual clues.

6. Notifications: Popup or toast messages that alert users to things like fresh messages or updates.

Swiping, scrolling, and clicking, hovering over content, like, sharing, and saving, adjusting volume levels, muting and unmuting your phone, and the mall restroom faucet sensing your hand are all examples of micro-interactions or include them. Once you recognize the trigger-feedback relationship between them, it is simple to understand.

Let's explore the mechanism of micro-interactions in more detail.

Mechanism of micro-interaction.

THE MECHANISM OF A MICRO-INTERACTION

Micro-interactions are trigger-feedback pairs, as we now know.

But what precisely does that mean?

Micro-interactions follow a typical four-step process. Which are;

1. Trigger: The first micro-interaction is a trigger. The user or the system itself can start it. Clicking, swiping, scrolling, and other user-initiated activities are examples of micro-interactions; system-initiated triggers, on the other hand, occur when particular criteria are matched and the system decides to initiate a trigger. A pop-up

animation or a notification, for instance, could be system triggered.

2. Rules: specify what occurs after the trigger is engaged.

3. Feedback: After the trigger is pulled, everything the user hears, sees, or feels (like vibration), in general, counts as feedback. For instance, when you swipe, that acts as a trigger; the feedback is the animation you see on the screen (colors, highlights, or the screen altering in an animated way).

4. Loops & Modes: determine the meta-rules of the micro-interaction, they are needed when the conditions of the micro-interactions change. Although they might not have been included in the original design, they are crucial for customer happiness.

What Makes Micro-interactions Important?

Despite being referred to as micro-interactions, they have a MACRO impact on the design and user experience. You can use some websites and programs that you truly like, and you can use others just to get things done. The distinction is significantly impacted by the micro-interactions, even though we aren't even aware of it.

Yet why? How then?
They improve usability of the UI.

Micro-interactions are excellent for improving usability.Although they can be applied to a wide range of platforms and forms, it is clear that they are essential for user-friendliness. Most websites feature a tab bar that flashes when you hover over the icons, and some even create a new menu when you do so. Because it informs the user whether the tab bar or the icons are interactive or not, this micro-interaction is crucial. Although hearing can occasionally be just as important as seeing, our natural tendency is to focus on visual micro-interactions. Most of the time, a sound is also heard along with the notification. Without this kind of micro-interaction, I personally hardly ever recognize that I have received a notification.

They make the experience more enjoyable

I don't know about you, but if I hit a button on a terrible day and the button instantly transforms into a jet and takes off, I just feel a little bit better. Maybe think of Snapchat's bitmojis if you require a practical illustration. The bitmoji of the other party appears directly above your type bar while both parties are in the conversation and one is typing. That seems like a clever application of micro-interaction.

Snapchat Chat page showing Bitmoji micro-interactions.

They give it a more human touch.

We all have a small amount of anxiety about artificial intelligence; there is no need to deny it. We design and decorate software in an effort to make our apps and devices, well, less terrifying. For some reason, animated encounters seem less scary to the human mind. Most likely because they are adorable, but anything goes. Take a look at this artwork by Paarth Desai.

Notification icon (designed by Paarth Desai.)

Could this adorable bell ever cause you harm?

On a completely other (and less amusing) point, they actually make it more human. Consider all the outdated websites we used before micro-interactions became popular. Then there are those that you can currently access. We can all agree that visiting a website with poor design is torturous.

Users are encouraged to return.

Remember that a well-designed micro-interactions can and will carry out your promotion for you. Only a few micro-interactions manage to draw users in. It might be a little animation, like WhatsApp's trash bin animation for deleted voice recordings, or it might be something more substantial. Recently, Twitter developed a micro-interactions that shows several animations when a tweet is liked. They only needed to connect it to hashtags. Some individuals downloaded Twitter solely to see the trick once businesses and groups started creating their own animated hashtags. Micro-interactions draw in users and keep them around. We always return because they improve the user experience and make it enjoyable. Micro-interactions are critical, to put it plainly. But if you want to use them effectively, an epiphany won't cut it. Now let's talk about "how?"

How Do You Create Effective micro-interactions?

The majority of the time, we aren't even aware that we are engaging in a micro-interactions, but that is kind of the goal. A micro-interactions shouldn't overpower the entire design by grabbing all the attention. A well-designed micro-interactions is discrete, taking place in a split second or over the course of a lengthier interaction in an even more discrete manner. This is so even though users usually favor functionality over design, notwithstanding how much fun the design may be. Therefore, to improve user experience, micro-interactions should be instances where functionality and design collide.

If we were to examine an interaction more closely, we would find that micro-interactions have three key functions:

- Improve functionality and make it more enjoyable,
- Create a connection between the user and the design,
- And give the user a sense of direct control.

Animation offers the user a sense of control because they are aware of their control over the app as they receive feedback on their activities.

Additionally, because it's enjoyable to use, it forges a bond between the user and the design.

However, there is more to successful micro-interactions than that. There are dos and don'ts, and the line between them can occasionally be quite thin.

1. User pleasure is paramount

For a moment, let's start over from scratch.

Everything we do is with the user in mind.

The micro-interaction and the design's primary goal are to satisfy the user. With that in mind, it is now abundantly evident that micro-interactions need to be properly planned. Although the interaction appears to be working properly at first, it may really make things harder for users to utilize or worsen their overall experience.

2. Maintain simplicity

Micro-interactions. are essential since they improve usability in the main.

So why make things difficult?

While using cute animations everywhere may not be the best idea, they are nonetheless cool. In addition, too much animation might harm a company's reputation. Keep it serious while having fun. Although it may be slight, the distinction nonetheless occurs.

3. Avoid letting it overpower the information.

This is crucial, especially if your product isn't the actual website or app. Returning to the Twitter example, only one tiny micro-interaction caused everyone to go insane. However, since Twitter's product is the app itself and the firm as a whole is quite large, it didn't have a negative impact on Twitter. But picture a business that sells things experiencing the same way. Despite being effective marketing, the product itself is still overshadowed. Such "marketing" is not always dependable or consistent because users won't remain on your website or app forever, and in the end, it could negatively impact you.

4. You don't need it if it doesn't work.

Some websites and applications make the error of using numerous design elements just for aesthetic purposes. You need to keep in mind your product and what it can do in situations like this. You don't really need an interaction that informs the user of the time if you sell sneakers. Only the necessary interactions should be kept, and they should be improved.

5. Avoid creating a new wheel.

Users are used to specific kinds of interactions, whether those interactions take place with digital or physical devices. Think about starting an app and scrolling down, for instance. If the page moved up instead of down, wouldn't you be momentarily confused and perhaps even irritated? We are all used to things functioning the opposite way, which is why. Utilize tradition while being revolutionary at the same time. When a little bit of the new is added to the old, it can sometimes be good enough.

A good example of micro-interactions.

Night/Day Mode
Let's examine my all-time favorite micro-interactions.

Sincerely, I have no idea how I endured the bright theme in the past.

Bravo to whoever thought of the dark mode!

Check out these examples right now. It's a good switch interaction by Andrey Bogdanov. Although I particularly like the moon-sun changeover, the absence of "light-dark" tags makes it somewhat perplexing.

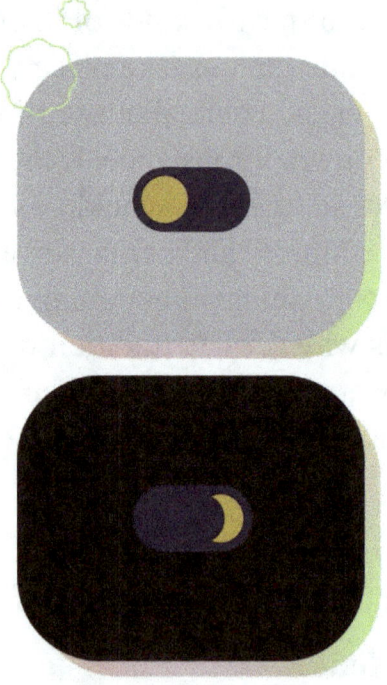

Night and Day mode switch. (designed by Andrey Bogdanov)

Micro can become gigantic in UX design. Micro-interactions can last only a few milliseconds, yet their impact on the user experience cannot be disputed. A single effective animation or sound design can hook users, whilst a poor design can turn them off. Additionally, these minor occurrences have marketing value. Even yet, those little moments can be challenging. One needs to develop the ability to tweak their subtlety and relevance to the rest of the product. The weight of making all of these decisions falls on the UX designer, but it is really just the power to employ the most potent tool available in the digital world.

Effective micro-interactions strengthen users' emotional bonds with a product in addition to being utilitarian. When carefully thought out, even seemingly insignificant features can have a significant impact on customer pleasure and the overall success of a digital experience.

A/B TESTING

Split testing, sometimes referred to as A/B testing, is a potent technique for user experience (UX) design and improvement. In order to establish which performs better in terms of user engagement, conversion rates, or other important metrics, two versions of a website, app, or product—designated as A and B—must be compared. A/B testing allows for data-driven decisions to enhance UX and accomplish particular objectives. You can gather information about the effects of changes to your website or app by doing an A/B test that directly contrasts a variant against the current experience. This allows you to ask targeted questions regarding the changes.

Testing removes the element of guesswork from website optimization and makes data-driven decisions possible, changing the tone of company dialogues from "we think" to "we know." You can make sure that every adjustment has a good effect by tracking how it affects your stats.

The process of A/B testing

A/B testing involves altering a webpage or app screen to produce a second version of the same page. A single headline, button, or a complete page redesign can all be included in this modification. Then, half of your traffic sees the page as it originally appeared (known as the control or A) and half sees the page as it has been modified (known as the variation or B).Visitors are shown with either the control or variation, and their interaction with each is tracked, gathered on a dashboard, and then analyzed using a statistical engine. After that, you can assess if altering the experience (variation or B) had a favorable, unfavorable, or neutral impact in comparison to the initial experience (control or A).

Reasons to conduct A/B tests

A/B testing enables people, groups, and businesses to modify their user experiences with care while gathering information on the results. This enables them to generate hypotheses and discover which aspects and experience optimizations have the most influence on user behavior. Another technique to disprove them is with an A/B test, which can disprove their belief that a particular experience is the optimal one for achieving a particular goal. A/B testing can be used to gradually improve a specific experience or a specific objective like conversion rate optimization (CRO) rather than merely addressing a one-time query or resolving a dispute.

A B2B technology firm could wish to increase the quantity and quality of sales leads coming from campaign landing pages. The team would try A/B testing adjustments to the headline, subject line, form fields, call-to-action, and overall layout of the page in order to optimize for a lower bounce rate, more conversions and leads, and a higher click-through rate. They can identify which modifications had an impact on visitor behavior and which ones did not by testing one change at a time. They can eventually aggregate the effects of several successful experiment-based adjustments to show how a new experience is measurably superior to the old one. This approach to making adjustments to a user experience enables the experience to be optimized for a desired result and can increase the effectiveness of key phases in a marketing campaign. Marketers can discover which versions of ads generate more clicks by tweaking the copy. They can discover which design is most effective at converting people into clients by evaluating the ensuing landing page. If every component of each phase contributes as effectively as feasible to the acquisition of new clients, the entire cost of a marketing campaign may even be reduced. Product designers and developers can utilize A/B testing to show how new features or modifications to a user experience will affect sales. A/B testing can be used to improve product onboarding, user engagement, modals, and in-product experiences as long as the goals and the hypothesis are clearly established.

A/B TESTING METHOD

An A/B testing framework that you may use to begin conducting tests is as follows:

Gather data: Your analytics platform, such as Google Analytics, can frequently offer guidance on where to start optimizing. To enable you to collect data more quickly, it can be helpful to start with high traffic regions of your website or app. Make sure to seek for sites with high bounce or drop-off rates that can be enhanced for conversion rate optimization. To uncover other areas for development, check out polls, social media, and other sources like heatmaps.

Establish goals: The metrics you'll use to gauge whether the variant is more effective than the original version are known as your conversion goals. Goals can range from making a purchase of a product to simply clicking a button or link.

Create test hypotheses: to explain why you believe you're a/B testing ideas will be superior to the existing version once you have determined your aim. When you have a list of suggestions, order them according to predicted impact and implementation difficulties.

Make various variations: Make the required adjustments to a component of your website or mobile app using you're a/B testing tools (such as Optimize Experiment). This could involve customizing anything totally, such as altering the color of a button, rearranging the items on a page design, or hiding navigational features. A visual editor is available in many popular A/B testing software, which will make these modifications simple. To ensure that the various versions of your experiment behave as intended, run a test run.

Run the experiment: Start it, then watch for participants to join in! At this point, users of your website or app will be randomized at random to either the control experience or a variation of it. Each participant's performance is evaluated by measuring, tabulating, and comparing it to the baseline.

Await the test results: It may take some time to get a suitable result depending on the size of your sample size (the target audience). When an experiment's findings are reliable and statistically significant, you can tell by its results. Otherwise, it would be difficult to determine whether your adjustment had a genuine effect.

Analysis of outcomes is necessary when your experiment is over. You're a/B testing program will present the experiment's data, show you how the two versions of your page performed differently, and determine whether there is a statistically significant difference between them. It's crucial to obtain statistically significant results so you may be sure of the test's outcome.

Congratulations if your entry is chosen as the winner. Check to see if you can use the experiment's lessons on other pages of your website and keep refining the experiment to get better results. Don't worry if your experiment yields no or a negative result. Create new hypotheses to test and use the experiment as a learning opportunity. Whatever the results of your experiment, make use of what you learned to guide future research and keep refining the user experience of your app or website.

A/B TEST OUTCOMES

Your goals will change depending on the kind of website or app you're testing. A B2B website may conduct more tests to optimize for leads, whereas a retail website might run more tests to optimize for purchases. The sort of website or app you are using will also affect how your results appear. Usually, the objectives are decided upon before the A/B test begins and are assessed at its conclusion. Some A/B testing systems let you modify your tests' objectives after the experiment has been completed or peep at findings as they come in real-time. Two (or more) versions, their respective audiences, and target completions are displayed on a test results dashboard. A typical view might include visitors, clicks, and a conversion rate, which is the proportion of visitors who converted. Let's say you optimize for clicks on a call-to-action (CTA) on a website.

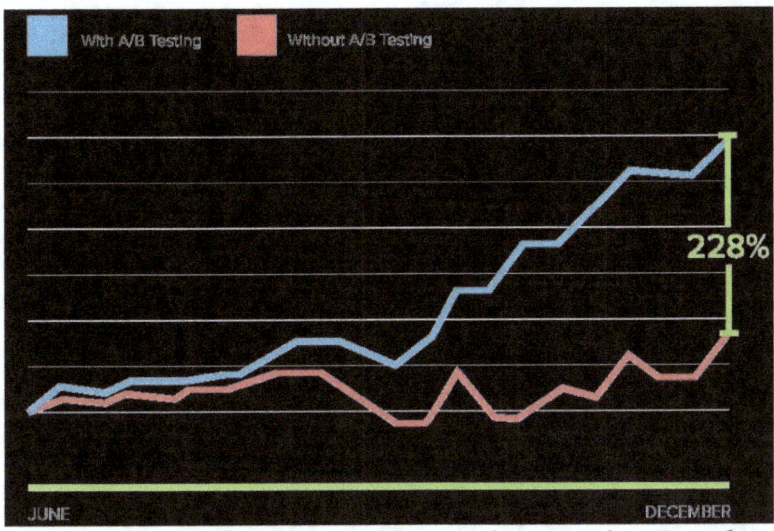

Statistical graph showing improvement of a particular site with A/B testing

A/B TEST SEGMENTATION

For their A/B tests, larger websites and apps frequently use segmentation. This is a useful technique to test modifications for particular groups of visitors if your site has a large enough number of visitors. Separating new from returning visitors is a typical segment for A/B testing. This enables you to test modifications to elements, such as signup forms, that only apply to new visitors.

On the other hand, selecting too small of an audience for tests is a typical A/B testing error. As a result, it may take some time before statistically significant data are obtained and it is possible to determine the effect of your change on a certain group of website users. To avoid false positives, it is crucial to measure the size of your segments before beginning an experiment.

SEO AND A/B TESTING

A/B testing is permitted and encouraged by Google, which also claims that there is no inherent harm to your website's search engine ranking when you do A/B or multivariate tests. However, utilizing an A/B testing tool improperly for things like cloaking could put your search rank in danger. In order to prevent this, Google has provided some best practices:

- No cloaking: The practice of giving search engines content that is different from what a typical visitor would see is known as cloaking. Cloaking may lead to the demotion or removal of your website from the search results. Avoid abusing visitor segmentation to show Googlebot alternative content based on user-agent or IP address to avoid cloaking.

- Use the rel="canonical" property to link variations back to the original version of the page if you're conducting a split test with several URLs. By doing this, you can reduce the chance that Google-bot will become baffled by many iterations of the same page.

- Use a 302 (temporary) redirect rather than a 301 (permanent) redirect when running a test that changes the original URL to a variation URL. Search engines like Google are informed by this that the redirect is temporary and that they should continue indexing the primary URL rather than the test URL.

➢ A media company might wish to attract more readers, lengthen readers' visits to the site, and encourage social sharing of its content. They might experiment with different versions of:

- Sign-up forms for emails
- Recommended resources
- Buttons for social sharing

➢ A travel agency can wish to boost the quantity of successful bookings made through their website or mobile app, or they might want to boost ancillary sales revenue. They might experiment with different versions of:

- Modals for homepage searches
- Results page for a search
- Additional product display

➢ An online retailer can wish to enhance customer satisfaction in order to boost holiday sales, the average order value, or the number of completed checkouts. They may do an A/B test to achieve this:

- Website promotions
- Navigational aids
- The parts of the checkout funnel

➢ A technology company may wish to raise the quantity of high-quality leads for their sales team, boost the amount of people who sign up for a free trial, or draw in a certain kind of customer. They might examine:

- Fields for lead forms
- Flow of free trial signups
- Calls to action and messaging on the homepage

Benefits of optimization and A/B testing include:

1. Data-Driven Decision Making: A/B testing gives empirical proof of which design decisions or adjustments improve user experiences and results.

2. Continuous Improvement: A/B testing promotes an iterative method of design and optimization, supporting continuous advancements.

3. Efficiency: It reduces wasteful effort by allocating resources to design improvements that are likely to have a favorable impact.

4. Reduced Risk: Decisions based on data are less likely to result in design modifications that have a detrimental impact on user engagement.

5. User-Centric: To make sure that design decisions are in line with user needs, A/B testing concentrates on user behavior and preferences.

6. Increased Conversion Rates: Optimization based on the outcomes of A/B tests can result in higher conversion rates, better user retention, and higher income.

7. Individualization By adjusting the UX to specific user segments, A/B testing may also be utilized to create tailored content or experiences.

A/B testing is a flexible technique used in marketing, product development, and other areas in addition to UX design. Organizations may continuously improve user experiences, achieve corporate goals, and stay competitive in a dynamic digital market by methodically testing and optimizing design features and elements.

CONCLUSION

We have journeyed through the pages of this book to examine the complex world of User Experience (UX) design—a field where empathy and empathy meet creativity, and technology and psychology interact. We've dived deeply into the art and science of creating digital experiences that resonate with users, leaving a lasting mark on their hearts and minds, from the fundamental principles to the most cutting-edge methods. As we come to the end of our journey, it is abundantly evident that UX design is about people, not just about pixels and code. It involves comprehending their requirements, anticipating their wants, and developing solutions that seamlessly fit into their daily life. It involves providing experiences that inspire happiness, simplicity, and delight.

The Laws of UX, the importance of understanding user psychology, the influence of cognitive psychology on design, and the complex dance of emotions in user experiences have all been revealed in this book. We've looked at how UX design has changed over time, how mobile has become increasingly important, and how important accessibility and inclusion are. We've covered microinteractions, information architecture, navigation, A/B testing, and optimization's transformational potential. The journey does not, however, finish here. UX design is a dynamic, always changing field. The expectations of users also grow as technology does. One must adopt a culture of constant learning, innovation, and user-centricity if they want to be at the forefront of this sector. As designers, developers, and creators, it is our duty to not only create digital products but also to mold experiences that have lasting value. Designing with purpose, empathy, and the steadfast conviction that every user deserves an easy, delightful experience while navigating the digital world are key components.

So, as you explore the realm of UX design, let this book serve as your compass. Let its knowledge spark your imagination, direct your choices, and serve as a constant reminder that the heart of design beats to the beat of human experience. You have the ability to design outstanding user experiences, make technology available to everyone, and leave a legacy of enduring, meaningful encounters. Your designs—designs that don't merely exist but also thrive, resonate, and transform—are what the world is waiting for.

Now, make whatever you want. Your users are eagerly anticipating your magic touch.